Disarmed

Disarmed

From McDonald's to the Frontlines with NCIS,
One Woman's Quest for Workplace Equality

ROBYN COLEMAN

ISBN: 9781979714228 (paperback)

Contributions by Thomas McCarthy
Edited by Elite Authors
Cover Design by Elite Authors
Layout by Thomas McCarthy
Photographs by Robyn Coleman

To my loving husband, mother, father, and sister for always being supportive in all my endeavors; for always motivating me; and for always being a voice of reason. You all have always been my biggest advocates.

To my children, to include my fur baby (Charley), for the unconditional love and joy you unknowingly give me each and every day. Thank you for giving purpose to my life.

To my extended family, for being a part of my life journey. From my aunt that influenced my career path to the cousins that benchmarked my childhood, you have and still are an integral part of who I am today.

To my friends from all over the world, you have etched a special place in my heart. I am forever grateful for the moments we have shared together, and look forward to the experiences we will share in the future.

A special thank you to Thomas McCarthy for his vision and contributions to this book. You have always believed in the power of my story. Through this journey, you have been a mentor and a newfound friend. I appreciate the countless hours you spent answering my questions and your patience throughout the years.

To all those that were an inspiration, good or bad, in my life—coworkers, associates, the insignificant others and exes, etc.—there was something learned from our encounters with each other, whether positive or negative; those experiences have made me wiser and a better person overall.

To the slew of doctors, psychiatrists, psychologists, and therapists I have seen since leaving government service, you have saved me! Without your guidance and your sensible influence, I would not be where I am today. Thank you for allowing me to speak my truth without judgement.

And to all the women that have faced adversities in the workplace—who felt they had no voice and/or experienced reprisal for speaking out—you are not alone; this book is for you.

CONTENTS

PROLOGUE

I had lost track of time, but the cold from the unforgivingly hard tile floor crept steadily through my flight suit, rising and slowly penetrating my legs. It had been hours since we left the safety of the small Marine camp in the brown desert haze of the Iraqi winter. Shivering, tense, crouched in this complete stranger's house after what had been a long foot patrol from Rawah, I felt the staccato bursts of gunfire spark a question I had repeatedly asked myself: What the hell am I doing here?

I did take some small comfort from the Marines who surrounded me while we waited for the explosives unit to arrive and recover some ordnance that had been found in the suspected terrorist's home where we now took shelter.

But they were still hours away, and there was nothing to do but wait.

Multiple bursts of gunfire seemed to surround us, like they were coming from next door. I was comforted to some extent from the protection offered by the adobe and tile of our temporary two-story shelter. And to a lesser extent, I tried to believe repeated assurances from the Marines that it was only "friendly fire."

I did know this: I wasn't in Cincinnati anymore.

I was on yet another mission as a lead criminal investigator for the NCIS, a woman in the testosterone-driven world of young men in combat. I was maybe the first woman they'd seen in days if not weeks. It was an edgy, tense, and often unpredictable world, where despite my uniqueness, I felt comfortable if slightly out of place, confident in my skills as we waited for the explosives unit to disarm the bomb that now sat in its lethal cradle upstairs.

I was part of a team that included not only the Marines but an interpreter and another law enforcement professional, a contractor who acted as a civilian adviser for the military.

I was the only woman that cold morning waiting for the explosives unit, but I felt like one of the guys—my hair pulled back in a bun under my Kevlar helmet, no makeup, rifle slung over my shoulder, gloves covering my feminine hands. We all looked the same in our Kevlar and khaki. When I look back on my NCIS career now, I often think if I had dressed in that gender-neutering uniform in the office, none of the men in charge would have known and wouldn't have treated me any differently from "the guys."

But of course the subtle differences were lost on the Marines. Before we left camp, I had drained my bladder and put in a tampon because I was menstruating. I had stuffed a pocket with panty liners and brought an extra wad of toilet paper. I never wanted to have the Marines feel I was a burden.

The Marines were with me that morning to provide protection while I investigated the site. We had nothing to do but wait tensely for the explosives unit to arrive, release the Marines, and retrieve the painstakingly constructed bomb. Bombs like that had killed and maimed too many of our troops, too many innocent Iraqis. I took some small amount of satisfaction in knowing that I had had a role in making sure the bomb upstairs would do no damage to anyone or anything. But I still had to sit there. It could be hours, and while we waited the interminable wait, I couldn't help but think that at any moment, terrorists could descend on us, charge the house, and kill everyone. Rape me.

At first, we had stood outside the house, but as darkness descended, every window and rooftop became a potential opportunity for an enemy kill shot, and we moved inside, hoping we could use the suspected terrorist's family as a shield.

Crouched on that cold floor, surrounded by Marines, waiting, it hit me.

Whether it was from nervousness or a full bladder, I had to pee. But that would have to wait.

It had already been a long night as I watched the Marines take turns standing guard outside. At one point, I saw some women and children in another room, and I noticed they all stared at me, amazed. I couldn't help but wonder what the women thought of me. Did they notice I was a woman? Did they see me as a terrorist invading their home?

Sleep was impossible with suspected terrorists in the next room. A man who looked to be the family's head slept in the hallway outside the room where we hunkered down waiting for the explosives team, as if he could block us and protect his family.

It's funny, I thought as I sat there. I had a rifle over my shoulder, a pistol on my hip, and hours and hours of extensive, painstaking cover-every-scenario training, yet nothing could have prepared me for this. This was the real thing, not a training exercise.

As the hours crept by, my eyes began to get heavy, as did all my protective gear. The weight of the Kevlar vest pressed rudely against my spine; I was tired, hungry, and frightened, and even in the middle of the Marines, I felt alone.

Are we even doing the right thing over here? I thought.

Finally in the distance I heard the comforting rumble of the Humvees and the mine-resistant armored MRAPs bearing the explosives team as daylight crept into our temporary shelter. We would be free to head back to Rawah soon, then grab a short helo hop back to Al Asad.

▲ ▲ ▲

On the trek back, my whole body felt like it was gliding on air. I couldn't wait until I could finally find sleep on my hard green military cot back at the base, another thing I would have found hard to believe not too long before.

A few days after that mission, a woman fully clothed in black detonated an explosives suicide vest at the entrance to the camp, killing herself and wounding several bystanders.

My time in Iraq coincided with many similar incidents. In January 2008, a month after I arrived, a suicide bomber killed thirty people at a home where mourners were paying respects to the family of a man killed by a car bomb. In early February, sixty-five more were killed when two female suicide bombers attacked a crowded market in eastern Baghdad. Later in February, more than fifty people heading to a Muslim shrine in Karbala were killed in another suicide attack.

I often thought about the attack outside our base and those later ones and realized quite suddenly what the women in the house that night thought of me: I was just another American in their land, and if they could have, they would have done whatever was necessary to me and to those Marines who sat with me that night to protect their beliefs, their family, and their country.

I was doing my job, a job I had quickly grown to love and would be very good at. In Al Asad, on my first overseas tour, surrounded by the terror and the bombs, I did not know that in the coming years I would be making some sacrifices as well. I, too, would have been willing to do anything to protect my job and myself. I did not know in that first glow of success that I would not be able to do anything about it.

Rawah Iraqi Police Station on March 17, 2008.

Inside Humvee somewhere in Iraq.

One

Before the Journey Begins

I wasn't prepared for it, which is fairly surprising, since I had spent my whole life preparing for things. I was confident—never cocky or overconfident or full of myself, but confident in the self-assured way that comes with doing well in school, working hard, and seeing a glimpse of the benefits that come along with all of that. I hadn't been handed anything, that's for sure, except maybe loving and encouraging parents and a few serendipitous breaks along the way. But that's how it's supposed to unfold: you make your own luck.

At any rate, I was barely a year out of the University of Cincinnati, making more money than I had imagined, and certainly a lot more than many of my college friends were making then. When I look back, at that point, quite a few of them still hadn't even found their first "real" jobs.

But there it was. After what was an exciting and, in a way, invigorating internship as a student inspector with the US Postal Inspection Service (USPIS) during my senior year, I was offered a full-time job with the group as a contract fraud analyst. I hadn't even graduated yet, but that is what I point to as "making your own luck." I volunteered for the internship, I did well, and they offered me a job. I still had to attend classes to graduate, which was extremely important to me. For a while, it was a bit crazy—I was working full-time at USPIS, going to class, taking exams, and getting ready to graduate. But I'm good at crazy, and everything went smoothly. I had a job that I think a lot of my criminal-justice-major friends at school would have slapped themselves silly to get.

And I took it, of course, and loved it. As I said, the money was good, and it was a real job, a good job. A year into that first real job, my supervisor, Gordon Silverman, urged me to take it to the next level and jump-start my career by applying to the Postal Service's Office of the Inspector General to work as a special agent. If I got the job, it would be a step up, and I would become a sworn federal law enforcement officer who carried a gun. Gordon made a few phone calls, I applied, and a few months later, I became the first USPS-OIG special agent in the Cincinnati office. I got my gun, and I got an entirely new level of responsibility.

In the ensuing years, across the globe, in combat zones and routine jobs in the States, investigating the grisly, analyzing the routine, dodging mortars and bureaucrats, I would always carry a gun. Until things well beyond my ability to control them anymore made it necessary for people to take my guns away.

I was twenty-two years old when I got the special agent's job. A huge responsibility? Yes. Daunting? Absolutely not.

Eventually two other seasoned special agents transferred to the Cincinnati office. One, Connie H., became a true friend and a gracious and patient mentor, even though I was fifteen years younger than her and my other colleague.

At first, I loved it. I loved the responsibilities and the challenges and the steep learning curve. I absolutely could not wait to get to work. I rarely needed coffee I was so hyper and intent on the job.

But as with many jobs with limited scopes—I mean there were only so many things we could investigate—I eventually became bored. I wanted something more challenging and more exciting than tracking down postal workers who were helping themselves to cash in the mail or claiming bad backs and looking for settlements.

Working there was a job that had satisfied many of my older colleagues at work. It was steady, certain, predictable, and routine.

But that was the problem. It was a job for people who were contented to be settled, who wanted the predictability and the lack of excitement. People who could pay their mortgages, go home every night to their kids and spouses, and enjoy the security.

But what I found, at twenty-two years old and a year into that job (and what I wasn't prepared for), was that I was bored to tears. All that security and predictability and day-to-day sameness was boring. It wasn't what I had imagined and what I had dreamed of.

It dawned on me at some point that many of my older coworkers were ready to ride the steady wave to retirement when I had just arrived at the beach and barely gotten my feet wet. I wanted something more exciting, a chance to travel, to be challenged, to get away from Cincinnati.

To do something.

I had always enjoyed challenges, whether it was classes at school or adapting to the normal tensions of being a teenager and facing peer pressure or dance team competitions or working after school at McDonald's. Whatever those challenges were, I met them and enjoyed myself at the same time.

I grew up in the Cincinnati area in Colerain Township and lived in the same comfortable house in a comfortable neighborhood on Spruceway Drive until I was eighteen. Both my father's and mother's families were big and extended and loving and supportive—six aunts and six uncles, which of course led to a slew of cousins.

My grandfather Coleman is out of the Deep South, from Andalusia, Alabama. He was and still is one of the most stubborn and frugal men I've ever met, and I love him dearly. I still cherish a trip we took—just him and me—to Andalusia when I was in my teens. I enjoyed helping him drive down there, but more than anything I enjoyed the one-on-one conversations, which didn't happen that often. He had seen a lot and been through a lot, yet was calm and confident. That was a Coleman trait I'm very glad I had inherited. In later years, it served me well. Growing up, we'd stay over at my grandparents' house, and my grandfather would just drive me and my sister around or treat us to his homemade ice cream. My mouth still waters thinking about it.

I still get a kick out of the time I badgered him to drive us to Kroger's down the street to get us some Twizzlers and we had a bad accident that did some serious damage to my grandfather's car. Even now he tells me it was the most expensive candy he's ever bought.

The Boykins, my mother's side of the family, were loud and boisterous and fun and great to hang out with—especially on big occasions—Fourth of July, Labor Day, Martin Luther King Day, Grandpa Boykin's birthdays. The parties were so much fun even strangers would show up to hear live music and get a taste of my Uncle Art's goat stew—fun, food, music, and games. And loud, with my aunts and uncles all trying to get their points across as the noise picked up amp by amp. But that's how the Boykins communicate.

Though the Boykins originally hailed from South Carolina, their Boykins roots went deep in that area of southwestern Ohio. The church I attended as a girl—and the one I still go to when I'm back in Cincinnati—was built by my Grandfather Boykin.

My parents worked hard and made sure my sister and I saw the value of doing the same. They're both still active. In fact, even though my dad has re- tired from GM, where he worked for years, he still works from time to time to pick up extra money for his "toys"—rebuilding old cars. And my mom ran an in-house day care from the time I was a little girl (after my sister was born); she now volunteers for non-profit organizations around Cincinnati.

▲ ▲ ▲

Did I have a picture-book childhood? Yes. I believe I did. It was not without its tensions and problems, certainly, but I'd have to say it was pretty good. And a pretty good childhood can provide a solid base on which to grow as an adult. And that helped me later, in Iraq, in Afghanistan, and a few other places in between. When the tensions first crept into daily life while I was in Djibouti, I drew on the strengths I had absorbed as a child simply by being wrapped in the embraces of a loving family. The lessons I learned as a young girl were implicit. There was never any "this is what you do" sort of advice. The lessons I got at home and in church and growing up I got by simply observing or learn- ing from others' mistakes. Those lessons would help me immensely later. But even those lessons lost their strength in the darkest of days later.

School was another thing that I think made me stand out a bit. As I said, I was always fairly confident in myself, a personality trait that would spark a great deal of trouble when I was with NCIS. Confident women were not exactly what many of the guys were comfortable with.

My parents really stressed education, and until I finished eighth grade, I attended private schools, first Beautiful Saviour Lutheran School, just down the street from Spruceway, then Calvary Christian Academy in Springdale until eighth grade. I started first grade at five because my mother talked the school board into it.

My parents earnestly wanted me to have better opportunities than they had, so they tried to give me the best education available. And the fact of the matter is, I absolutely loved private schools, I think because they focused on education (and because we didn't have any of the social distractions, like school dances or outside activities or clubs, and because we wore uniforms. What trendy clothes to wear wasn't something I worried about).

But the crunch came when I went to public school and started at Northwest High. First, because I was younger than most of the incoming freshman and second, because I was the target at first for some razzing because of the way I dressed. It's hard to develop a great daily fashion sense when you've been wearing uniforms for eight years of school. I still remember one boy, LaDon, making fun of my shoes and overhearing Kathie B. mocking a yellow dress I'd worn with a black turtleneck. She said I looked like a bee. Silly stuff, for sure.

But here is the interesting thing that perspective and maturity and hard-earned experience can give anyone. That adolescent, peer-pressure, infantile silliness, the stuff of fourteen- and fifteen- and sixteen-year-old children? It made some of the things I would go through later at NCIS seem mature and thoughtful.

In the end, I got over that fairly quickly, and in the end, I was very comfortable not being part of any peer group, just being myself. In fact, I hung around with everyone *but* the popular kids. I just wasn't into getting status by hanging out with the cool set. Let's put it this way: I wasn't going to be elected prom queen or most popular anything. And I was truly fine with that.

And I probably didn't do myself any favors by being a teacher's pet in a couple classes and working in the school office. Mr. Alteri, my history teacher, always favored me and had me write out his notes during every class; he told me it was because of my penmanship—and he'd tell the class how neat my writing was. That's the kind of student I was: popular with the teachers and staff, but not so much with the other students. But the fact is I really didn't care. My focus was on being successful.

In fact, I made the varsity dance team every year. But in my junior year, none of my friends were moved up from JV. So I just stepped back down to JV. I'd rather have been with them.

So even though it was an adjustment, high school was a time of focus for me, and I made the honor roll and the National Honor Society, had perfect attendance, and was actually part of an elite student group, the Senior Honors Seminar, my senior year. And I worked at McDonald's after school and during the summers did professional leadership programs at Miami University in Oxford, Ohio and the College of Mount St. Joseph in Cincinnati.

I loved my job at McDonald's. Sometimes I think it was the best job I ever had, and in moments of wistfulness, I think I should go back there. It was my first real tax-paying job, at the restaurant on Boymel Drive in Fairfield, Ohio. I was fifteen, younger again than any other employees—a pattern you might notice developing.

I think what made the Boymel Avenue McDonald's so great was the team we had. I loved the crew I worked with and loved coming to work. The camaraderie there was crazy—we all just got along. I worked there on and off all the way through my second year in college, if you can imagine that. But that's how much I loved it. By the time I left, I could run every station: drive-through, cashier, grill, dishes, and front counter. The only thing I did not do was unpack the truck.

Another interesting thing as I look back on those days, colored by my experiences with supervisors in later more responsible jobs, was my managers. I loved them because they always made me feel a part of the team. I'm not sure how well it would go over with Washington, DC, bureaucrats, but I think anyone in government positions of leadership would be well served by taking a few classes at McDonald's Hamburger University. Maybe that wouldn't go over so well, but it would do wonders.

Our group dynamics at that little McDonald's would have made some of the NCIS groups I worked with later blush with envy. We had Simeon and Mike close grill because they could do it blindfolded, while I busted out dishes because I was pretty fast. We had a guy named Lurch—who looked like the character by that name from the *Addams Family* TV show—who cleaned the grease vats and cleaned the bathrooms. He loved the nickname, too, and lived up to it in a way because he drove a hearse as his everyday car. Because we all worked so well together, we would close in an hour flat. Afterward, the whole night crew would go to Denny's to hang out and just talk. We even did some group movies together and made sure everyone was taken care of.

▲ ▲ ▲

In high school, because other kids knew I was a good student, they'd often ask me for help, which I readily provided. But there were times when I felt as if other kids took advantage of me. Once a girl and her entourage actually accosted me during a study hall and demanded my homework.

I had a hard time telling people no. But I tried to lead a positive life and set a good example, and at times, I didn't even mind sacrificing a bit to help someone out. A therapist once told me later that I was a people pleaser. I think I always had been, until later—in my professional career and personal life— when I learned how to stand up for myself.

But all that high school drama aside, I graduated in 1999 at seventeen and headed off to Wright State University in Dayton, majoring in psychology.

We all have life-changing events, often something that provokes a crystal-clear, energizing moment of inspiration. Mine happened the next year when I took my aunt up on an invitation to join her at a Take Your Daughter to Work Day. That afternoon changed my life and gave me an almost laser-like focus on what I wanted to do.

My aunt Donna was at the time and is still today a successful woman. She had started out thinking about law school but somehow ended up as an administrator for the Ohio Department of Corrections. Since at the time I showed an interest in criminal justice, she offered to have me shadow her during a day while she was assistant director of the Talbert House, a halfway house on Reading Road in Cincinnati. Residents there, mostly drug offenders, were serving a period between prison and release back into society.

I was blown away, both by how the residents reacted to my aunt and also by the potential for a career in criminal justice. That day shadowing my aunt, I saw a woman who was a leader, whom people respected and deferred to, who was in charge and had that aura about her that brought people in.

I was inspired.

That was it for me, and I made up my mind right then and there that I wanted to take up criminal justice as a major.

I will never forget what she told me that day: if I worked in corrections, I would know exactly what I was dealing with because I could simply look at an offender's record. As I thought about it, I decided I'd pursue the law enforcement side rather than the corrections side because I decided I needed the fresh air and freedom. I didn't think I could handle being behind bars all day long—I wasn't a criminal. It would have driven me crazy.

And the totally ironic thing about my choice is that I'm not overly fond of cops, especially the local and state varieties. I think a lot of them are arrogant and feel entitled and above the law.

That's why, right from the start, I went for the federal side, which I felt had more substance, more meaning. At a federal agency, I'd be doing investigations that had a much greater and more far-reaching impact than the local and state cops, who just wrote tickets and harassed the public, I thought.

That day at Talbert House with my aunt, seeing how people reacted to her and how she calmly and almost stoically commanded such respect and attention, changed my life. It gave me a direction to go with my dedication. And the first thing I did was leave Wright State and my psychology major and move to the University of Cincinnati for a criminal justice degree.

I was on my way.

The University of Cincinnati, considered a top-tier school, is larger than one might think, with close to forty thousand students. But by the time I transferred, I'd finished all my general education coursework at Wright State and needed only to focus on criminal justice courses. I had nothing to distract me and soon worked my way into the internship with USPIS, then the full-time job. The downside: I still had to attend classes at night and work toward my bachelor's degree. The upside? I was twenty-one and pulling in a salary of some $60,000 a year.

I thrived in that environment, enjoyed the money of course, and enjoyed finally making my own way in the world at something that seemed to me to have great potential and possibly even some excitement. Not surprisingly, eighteen months after I graduated college, I had a full-time job as a criminal investigator.

In that job, officially I investigated "fraud, waste, abuse, and misman-agement" of the US Postal System. Specifically, that meant investigating Postal Service employees trying to get away with workers' compensation fraud, among other things. And that meant going over medical records, re-viewing confidential information, conducting surveillance operations, and reviewing other documents. Maybe it meant someone had put in a workers' compensation claim from lifting a heavy mailbag that had caused severe and permanently disabling back pain. And maybe that meant supervising a surveillance operation to observe that same employee playing golf with no problems.

Other typical investigations might cover mail theft by employees, things like stealing gift cards and cash from letters, or other types of financial fraud, such as stealing stamps.

But that would have been the exciting side of things. For the most part, my wonderful salary aside, it was repetitive work, and it was far from challeng-ing or stimulating mentally. As a new agent, I was ready to bust down some doors and get into some action. That just wasn't happening, and I felt fairly quickly that I needed and wanted something more.

We had perks that would make many people weep with joy—a take-home car, overtime, comp hours, work from home. These were wonderful benefits for someone with a family or someone looking down the road at retirement. But they didn't seem so wonderful to me, a still-wet-behind-the-ears new-comer, and I soon found myself dreading going to work, and worse, I found myself getting lazy in the predictable routines of the job.

I did have the opportunity to fall under the influence of a great mentor while I was there, though: Connie H., an awesome investigator with whom I worked with a lot. In fact, we were the only two women doing these investiga-tions in Ohio at the time, and we stuck together like glue, doing surveillance and interviews together. Connie was very smart and would be able to gently tell me if I had dropped the ball on something, which is the best if not the only way to learn.

Once, interviewing an employee suspected of forging a medical docu-ment, I simply froze up in the middle of trying to get her to confess. It was one of my first interviews fresh out of training, and I just froze. Connie was with me as a backup, read my body language, could see I was heading for trouble, and picked up the interview without missing a beat.

She got the confession, and on the ride home, she told me I had dropped the ball during the interview—but then assured me that things would get better with experience. She didn't scold but instead tried to reassure me. I still look up to her for what she did to help me when I was so new.

Another benefit was the training I received as a special agent, which provided me with the opportunity to get federal government investigation training, which in turn got me the certification I needed to make a lateral move into another agency if I wanted.

So it was that in June 2005 I was attending advanced interviewing classes at the Federal Law Enforcement Training Center in Glynco, Georgia, when I met two guys from NCIS. By that time, I had recognized my postal boredom and had started doing something about it, applying to jobs with the Secret Service, the FBI, and the DEA—anything that would expand my expertise beyond postal fraud. Both guys gave me the rundown about NCIS, and it sounded like it might be something I'd be interested in pursuing.

I'd always been a networker, and after that session, I networked like nothing I had done before. Once I decided to apply with NCIS, someone within NCIS hand delivered my application to someone else with connections in high places at NCIS headquarters in Washington, DC. I realized this seems almost far fetched, but believe me, that's how it works and what you almost need to do to get into these agencies. If you don't already have a government job, it's hard to get into the good ole boy network. You need to know somebody who knows somebody to penetrate the layer of bureaucracy. It's sad but true.

I've found over the years that in many cases, agencies already have someone in mind to hire for an advertised position before it is even advertised; they only advertise the position to avoid any equal opportunity or discrimination issues. Since I came from a law enforcement background and had the basic criminal investigations training, I was already more appealing to other special agent positions I applied to, and I moved along pretty quickly through their process.

Once I had my NCIS application in the works, I withdrew the other ones I had out there. But I also had other thoughts that made the NCIS much more appealing. DEA seemed too limited in its scope—just drugs—and the dangerous undercover work seemed a bit much. The Secret Service lost its appeal to me because it required five years on the presidential detail in Washington. And I realized that I cherished my life too much and as a result might not be the best person to take a bullet for someone else, president or not. I withdrew from the FBI process because its training center in Quantico, Virginia, outside Washington, didn't recognize the training I already had. It would have been like starting all over again.

▲ ▲ ▲

So it was NCIS or bust, and I settled in for the long application process, which took a year. By that time, at my networking best, I had already met Thomas Betro, the director of NCIS at the National Organization for Black Law Enforcement (NOBLE) conference in Cincinnati, where I was working a recruitment booth for the USPS-OIG—which I was "volunteered" for. Actually I was told to volunteer, since I was the only ethnic person in Ohio working for them in that capacity.

As it turned out, the NCIS recruitment booth was in the next aisle over, and I worked my magic and actually wound up meeting the folks handling my application. It was networking at its best. This bit of luck allowed me to drop in a comment about the seeming dead point I was sitting at in the application process, with nothing going on at the moment. Bingo!

Not long after the NOBLE conference, I received my conditional hiring notice from NCIS, and in December 2006, three years after graduating from the University of Cincinnati and six years after my fateful visit to the Talbert halfway house with my aunt Donna, I had opened yet another door. And it was a door that I hoped would allow me to see the world beyond Cincinnati and the USPS.

My Family (L to R: Robyn, Mother, Father, and Sister).

Paternal Grandfather—Calvin Coleman and his City of Cincinnati
Proclamation for "Coleman Family Day" on July 23, 2011.

Paternal Grandmother—Treva (née Blaine) Coleman.

Maternal Grandparents—James Boykin and Lillie Mae (née Woods) Boykin.

Two

The Journey Begins

When I decided to move on from my increasingly unfulfilling work at USPS-OIG and apply for what seemed to me a far more exciting opportunity with NCIS, I'd done enough research to know I had the background NCIS was looking for—and that I was the right age and had the college degree they wanted.

I knew I had done the networking dance as well as it could have been done, and I knew that my application had drawn the right attention from the right people.

What I didn't know, and was pleasantly surprised to learn, was that I also had a deep reservoir of patience. The process took forever. This is not in any way a criticism of NCIS but more an observation that if you want the security and benefits of a government job, you've got to be able to wait for it. And I mean wait.

It took more than a year from my first positive encounter, the first step, until I was actually able to tell my supervisor at the post office that I was leaving. It seemed interminable, but I was equipped for the wait and confident that it would all work out in the end—that I would get the NCIS job.

I learned while I was waiting that investigators had spoken with my colleague and mentor Connie—and with Daniel, my supervisor—because they both told me they'd given me glowing recommendations. Daniel was a lot of things, an interesting man, to say the least. But he was not a good manager. It was difficult at times to work for him, sometimes almost comical. But Daniel

15

never did anything that would be seen as mean spirited, condescending, or spiteful. Mostly he was just incompetent, which can happen in bureaucratic workplaces. Daniel knew how to play the game, how to get enough attention from the right people to keep being promoted, but he knew also to not do anything to call too much attention to himself. He kept on the radar, but he flew low. That's why he knew enough to speak highly of me. It reflected on his own management skills, or so he thought: I was a model employee because he was a terrific manager.

I knew investigators had also spoken to neighbors of my parents, because they quickly told my parents a strange person had been around asking questions about me. And of course investigators later talked to my parents.

Strangely, everything happened very quickly after waiting so long. The day I got the call, I was in my car in the USPS-OIG parking lot, trying to energize myself for another day, when the phone rang. It was a woman from NCIS offering me a job in California. I told the woman I'd call her back and immediately called Connie. I valued Connie's advice and her experience and her calm, thoughtful wisdom. She had already helped a great deal. Connie told me to take the job.

While I was waiting for that call, my biggest concern was my battle with boredom. I still took great pride in my job and kept learning, thanks to Connie. She knew I had applied to NCIS and had my back. And she continued to be a great mentor, something I remain grateful for to this day. She was always supportive, which is something anyone new on a job would relish.

Connie and I were the only women in the USPS-OIG office in the entire state of Ohio—a minority of two. And on top of that, we had Daniel, a supervisor from hell. Daniel was first and foremost a bureaucrat—a guy who had put in his time and kept his head down, didn't make waves, and slowly rose to the top. That's how it works. He was fluent in acronyms and procedures and forms. He could rattle them off and follow them to a tee, not unlike a robot. The other side of the picture, though, meant that he was a little short on the creativity and motivation meter.

And like any good bureaucrat, Daniel tended to be almost blissfully unaware of the needs and talents of the people around him and what they might be concerned about. It was always about the rules and proper procedures. He was not exactly enlightened when it came to male-female relations either. He was my first good ole boy boss. Not the last, but certainly a very memorable figure. But I have to say, compared with other supervisors I would have as I rose through the ranks at NCIS, Daniel was benign. He did not possess the viciousness or the jealousy that I would encounter later.

I never actually knew what Daniel did, just that I was surprised when he was promoted to supervisor. It just didn't make sense. It seemed to me that he was never there, and Connie and I would all too frequently be asked where he was. We never knew. I guess that's the magic of rising to the top. If you're not there, you can't annoy people. I think he genuinely believed the rules didn't apply to him. He did manage to make it into the office to leave enough of his 7-Eleven Big Gulps—those are thirty-two ounces of sugary craziness—to fill wastebaskets all over the office. I could never figure out where all the empty cups were coming from until Connie told me.

Daniel was also no stranger to good and plentiful meals, and he loved his cigars. Connie and I dreaded our quarterly trips to the regional office in Pittsburgh for training—a six-hour drive in good conditions. Daniel looked at these drives as an opportunity to speak at length to his captive audience of Connie and me. The only interruptions came when he took a long puff on his cigar. Needless to say, we kept the windows down as much as possible. I took great pains before those trips to time getting into the Ford Explorer for the drive so I could jump in the back seat at just the right moment. Thank God for the leg room in that vehicle. If we could have, both Connie and I would have been happy to let Daniel have the entire front seat to himself.

I have to say, I enjoyed giving Daniel my notice.

After I left for San Diego, I learned that Daniel had been fired, so to speak, which is an extremely difficult thing to accomplish in the USPS-OIG. I never did learn why, but to tell you the truth, I wasn't overly concerned. I did sometimes wonder why Connie wasn't promoted to supervisor before Daniel; she actually had more seniority than Daniel at the USPS-OIG. I never asked her feelings, but I wondered if she faced some similar scenarios during her career that I would later face.

I was content to keep working and dream about the next phase of my life.

The United States Naval Criminal Investigative Service, of course, has risen to public attention because of the television series, but the service has been around for a very long time—even before television and Mark Harmon.

NCIS is the primary law enforcement agency for the Navy. According to its official website, NCIS's mission is to "investigate and defeat criminal, terrorist, and foreign intelligence threats to the United States Navy and Marine Corps—ashore, afloat, and in cyberspace."

About half of the approximately 2,500 NCIS employees are civilian special agents trained to carry out a wide variety of assignments at locations across the globe. Among my later assignments were screening and investigating suspected terrorists in Iraq, and investigations of such things such as rapes and sexual assaults, thefts, unexplained deaths, suicides, and the gruesome and gritty crimes that can often occur when young men and women are living close together under extremely tense situations in places like Iraq and Helmand Province in Afghanistan, the deadliest place in a deadly country.

NCIS special agents are armed federal law enforcement investigators, who frequently coordinate with other US government agencies. NCIS special agents are supported by analysts and other experts skilled in disciplines such as forensics, surveillance countermeasures, computer investigations, physical security, and polygraph examinations.

It has been around under various names since 1892, when it was charged with collecting information on foreign vessels, charting foreign rivers and harbors, and collecting information on various overseas fortifications, industrial plants, and shipyards. Known as the Office of Naval Intelligence during World War I, its duties expanded to investigating possible threat of sabotage and espionage or other activities thought to be a threat to the Navy.

During the Cold War years—as Western and Soviet blocs challenged each other, the ONI saw the buildup of civilian special agents for the first time, and by 1992, NCIS had become a mostly civilian agency. By that time, its investigations of such things as the terrorist bombing of the Marine Barracks in Beirut in October 1983 that killed 299 American and French servicemen; the arrest of one of its own, Jonathan Pollard, for espionage; and the sexual misconduct of what became known as the Tailhook Scandal increased its public visibility.

NCIS agents were the first US law enforcement personnel on the scene of the attack on the USS *Cole*, and the American embassy in Mombasa, Kenya—precursors to the horrors of the events of Septembers 11, 2001. The first internet wiretap in the United States was performed by an NCIS agent.

NCIS agents are now stationed in more than 150 locations around the world.

Once I cleared the final application and security hurdles, my first posting for NCIS was to San Diego—clear across the country from Cincinnati, which was totally fine with me. I was incredibly ready to go, to leave Cincinnati, and to start a new phase of my life. Once I accepted the job, I focused on the move and didn't look back or question whether I had done the right thing.

It's funny, because I wasn't nervous about the move, or how I would fit in, or my abilities or training. I was actually more nervous about whether a federal program would buy my condo in Cincinnati, which it did.

I was ready for a new start and fired up to jump-start my ambitions to travel and become a more well-rounded agent. I had grown tired of the fraud investigations at the USPS-OIG and wanted to expand beyond what at times were predictable and easy-to-spot schemes that in the end didn't appear to be that well designed by the perpetrators. A hint to future postal workers: if you plan to grab a nice settlement from a claim that lifting heavy mailbags had rendered you nearly paralyzed, don't play golf three or four times a week, and maybe drop the gym membership. It still amazes me what people try to get away with.

I wanted more serious crimes. I wanted complications. I wanted details and puzzles and challenges. So of course, my first NCIS assignment in San Diego was on its fraud squad. Go figure.

Into the mix of the move and the changes and excitement I was also able to blend my boyfriend Leonard, known to all as Leo—a man I met and quickly fell for. Who wouldn't? I thought. Leo was handsome, funny, and built like a rock, which made sense because he had been an all-star athlete in high school. We had been dating for almost a year when I told him I had taken the NCIS job and was moving to California. He had been exceptionally supportive of my dreams and ambitions, which was wonderful.

Leo joined me in California shortly after I arrived in San Diego in December 2006, and I was overjoyed that he loved me enough to uproot his life in Cincinnati to continue our relationship. At the time, it seemed almost perfect.

By the time I arrived in San Diego, I had already taken the basic criminal investigation training with USPS-OIG in Glynco, Georgia, and that helped a bit. The course is intense and offers all federal employees a chance to start really digging in to what will be their new careers—an essential first step.

Its organizers consider it one of the most challenging aspects of law enforcement. We learned quickly that thorough and comprehensive investigations often yield successful criminal prosecutions—which in turn result in safer and healthier communities. For me, overseas, those communities would include US military bases in Al Asad, Iraq, Helmand Province, Afghanistan, and Camp Lemonnier in Djibouti. At the course, we learned that bringing a comprehensive case to prosecutors meant understanding and adhering to the core principles of the investigative process: the crime scene and how to manage it, take notes, and collect evidence. We learned the nuances of criminal Constitutional law, interrogation techniques—which would prove nearly priceless to me later—and how to write accurate and clear reports.

New NCIS hires with no federal training were required to go through twenty-two weeks of combined basic and advanced NCIS training. Because I had already taken and had actually excelled at the basic criminal investigation course, my training was cut to ten weeks. It included sexual assault training, firearms training, death investigations, protective service, and counterintelligence and counterterrorism training classes and practicals.

And while the basic course had already taught us some of these things, we of course had to learn the NCIS way of doing the more mundane things, such as writing reports, interviewing, and interrogating.

But the specific NCIS courses were terrific and exhilarating to me. All these various classes were taught in a way that put us right into the action: "What would you do in this situation?" These were teaching scenarios that proved to be a great way to learn—much better than lectures and textbooks. The training, I felt, was useful and very practical.

One thing that I relished and that became a part of my daily routine no matter where I was, was working out and keeping fit. I won the Distinguished Fitness Award in training, and it made me want to always strive to be the fittest female, no matter where I was assigned or what I was doing. As a woman in law enforcement, I never wanted to be seen as the weak link. Later, in San Diego, I became good friends with an agent, Josh, who was a total fitness junkie. He ate meticulously well and was ripped. I would always go to him with questions about nutrition and body fat in addition to workout tips.

Once I completed the necessary training and was in the field doing real-life work, I volunteered for anything, and I mean anything, that would give me some experience out of fraud. Need someone for a protective detail? Ask Coleman. How about help getting a search warrant? Coleman will do it.

I was the only black female in the San Diego office, so other agents would use me for different scenarios, which was great as far as I was concerned.

The first three months on the job called for shadowing an experienced agent, much the way a rookie cop would ride along with a veteran on a beat. And in my first three months, I saw a lot of action, which made me realize I had done the right thing leaving Cincinnati. I was in a high-speed chase that involved both NCIS agents and a San Diego police helicopter. We pinned the bad guy down at an intersection and had to call him out of his car as the helicopter hovered above. It was real drama, real action, and a very high-adrenaline experience—right out of a TV police drama, except it was real.

Another case saw me working with a crew serving a search warrant on someone suspected of possessing child pornography. I was covering the rear of the guy's house when other agents went in the front door, flushing him out the back wearing only his tighty-whitey Jockey shorts—and right into my waiting arms. I had him on the ground by the time the other agents arrived at the back of the house.

The hitch in all this was that to use "She'll Volunteer for Anything" Robyn Coleman, other agents would have to go through my boss, whom I'll call Jane. In the politest and most diplomatic language I can choose, I would have to say that Jane was a total and possibly certifiable annoyance. I was never certain if she was jealous or simply someone who like to cause tensions. I have learned, as has anyone who has ever worked in a job for any length of time, that some people simply thrive on creating problems. It is almost as if they derive some sort of backhanded energy from making other people squirm. I will never understand it, but it happens.

She tried to block every assignment other agents requested I help with. And if I volunteered to help on my own time (after my normal working hours), she told me she would still expect me to come in at regular schedule the next day: no comp time. In another irony of my career, I had left the male chauvinism of Daniel in Cincinnati and moved to a new job with a female supervisor, and she was just as bad.

But I dealt with Jane as I had dealt with Daniel—from a position of strength and confidence. I simply did what I was told, did it well, and never—under any circumstances—ever complained. I had been taught from the time I was a young girl that doing well is the best way to make a statement, and I held that belief close to my heart in everything I did.

There would come a time when I would begin to doubt the wisdom of that belief, but that would come later.

I have to say, though, that Jane was an equal opportunity shrew. At least two of my San Diego colleagues, agents I admired and had been learning from, volunteered for duty in Iraq to get out from underneath Jane's supervision. Imagine that. Iraq was not the most serene place on earth in 2006. And several other female agents left as well.

Outside of a few people, the San Diego office was a great introduction to NCIS. In fact, I still own a house there and plan eventually to return.

Unfortunately, one of those people was Jane. You can choose your job, you can research and study and network until you've exhausted all possibilities and covered every possible contingency. But in the end, you can't choose your boss. It's a game of chance, and for the second time, I rolled snake eyes. You just never know. Jane continually wrote me bad evaluations. It became predictable. But she did that for everyone she supervised, so I think getting a bad evaluation from her was not actually harmful. She certainly tried to block my attempt to volunteer for Iraq, but her efforts had no effect.

I somehow think her own supervisors realized something was wrong, given the stream of bad reports flowing from Jane and the unusual number of agents trying to escape her supervision.

A few years ago, long after I left San Diego, I heard she ran into trouble with the San Diego police and was demoted. I heard that later she resigned to prevent being fired.

I had to get away from Jane, and I had to get away from fraud. I wanted more than that. I wanted experience to round out my skills. That was why I left USPS-OIG for NCIS in the first place.

So, naturally, I volunteered for Iraq. Make sense? Probably not. But that is what I did. And to make it more emphatic, I volunteered for six months, not the usual four-month tour.

To make myself stand out a bit more, to be more attractive for the assignment when the "voluntary deployment" list came out, I stressed my training in advanced interviewing skills, something they were looking for. I learned later that bit of training did the trick. Because I was still what they considered a probationary agent—still wet behind the ears in my supervisors' eyes, and that included Jane—I did not get one single letter of recommendation or endorsement. And a small number of my colleagues told me I would never get the job; I was too new, they said.

But the fact is, they needed bodies in Iraq in 2006 and 2007, and for whatever reason, I was chosen.

When the list was posted, a much larger number of my colleagues than the few who had dismissed my chances earlier came up to me and congratulated me. At the time, I wasn't even sure what they were talking about. Then it hit me: I was going to Iraq.

I remember thinking, Thank you, Jesus. I'm getting away from Jane!

The audacity of what I had done, successfully volunteering and winning the assignment in Iraq, came home to roost as I was getting my inoculations, which among others included shots for smallpox, typhoid, tuberculosis, and anthrax.

Not something I needed in Cincinnati. I was headed for Al Asad, Iraq. My assignment? I would be part of a team investigating suspected terrorists, men captured by US troops in the confusing aftermaths of some of the most violent times in an increasingly violent war. Were they actual terrorists? Were they simply in the wrong place at the wrong time?

It would be my job to find out.

Homeland
Security

December 23, 2004

Robyn S.C. Coleman
United States Postal Service
Office of Inspector General
Covington, KY

Re: CITP-501

Dear Ms. Coleman:

Physical fitness is an important attribute for any law enforcement officer. It can have a real impact on an officer's ability to meet the many demands and responsibilities associated with the law enforcement profession.

You scored 90% or higher in all four areas of the Physical Efficiency Battery. This achievement qualifies you to receive the Distinguished Fitness Award for Criminal Investigator Training Program Class Number CITP-501. It is indeed a pleasure to award the enclosed certificate in recognition of your accomplishment of which you and your organization can be justifiably proud. Congratulations.

Sincerely,

Chief
Physical Techniques Division

Enclosure:
Certificate

www.fletc.gov

Federal Law Enforcement Training Center – "Distinguished Fitness Award" letter from December 23, 2004.

Federal Law Enforcement Training Center
Glynco, Georgia

Distinguished Fitness Award

This certifies that:

ROBYN S.C. COLEMAN

*Has completed the Physical Efficiency Battery [90%] Test obtaining
a score at the 90th percentile level or higher in the four evaluated areas of Flexibility,
Upper Body Strength, Speed & Agility and Cardiovascular Endurance. This certificate is
awarded in recognition of this physical fitness achievement.*

DECEMBER 23, 2004
Date

 Homeland Security

Chief, Physical Techniques Division

"Distinguished Fitness Award" certificate from December 23, 2004.

Protective service detail for an undisclosed party in San Diego, CA, on June 24, 2007.

Three

Al Asad

I left San Diego on a high that lasted for days and carried me through the seemingly never-ending flights halfway across the globe to Kuwait. From Kuwait, I would cross the border into Iraq and cross over into a new and dangerous world where US and NATO troops were still fighting a war that seemed without end—a war without a front line. Instead, pockets of resistance were everywhere throughout the country, and the enemy at times was difficult to determine. Stepping outside the confines of any fortified and protected base could be fatal.

But Iraq was where I would be helping and using my investigative and interrogation skills. That was what I was looking forward to—a meaningful and satisfying job where I would be making a difference. It was a heavy responsibility, though. If I erred one way, I might be sending an innocent man into the no-man's-land of Guantanamo Bay, Cuba, and years of prison. If I erred the other way, I might be setting free a terrorist who would return to build more roadside bombs and kill and maim more innocent civilians and our own troops.

I was up for it.

Our San Diego office Christmas party the afternoon before I left was a good start, and Leo and I enjoyed it immensely. We were serenaded in what I guess was a traditional Southern California way—with a mariachi band. At Christmas? Different, but nice.

After some enthusiastic good wishes and goodbyes from my colleagues, we left the party and later had a great dinner at a nearby Outback, where I gorged myself on Alaskan king crab—not something I thought would be in steady supply in the middle of the Iraqi desert. Then we went back home, watched videos, drank wine, and enjoyed our last night together. It was a wonderful and memorable evening, and I was grateful and happy the man I loved was so understanding of my need to explore and test my limits and get out and see the world.

Leo would watch the house, pay the bills, and keep things running while I was away, which was another thing I didn't have to worry about. Or at least I thought so at the time. I was ready.

Part of my NCIS training before I left involved "high-risk operations," which totally immersed me in certain aspects of things I'd be doing in Iraq. We had weapons training and drills with Mark 18s, shotguns, and other high-powered rifles. I loaded so many magazines on so many weapons I ended up having to tape my thumbs because they were so sore. We drove through obstacle courses set up in desert scenery in total darkness, learning how to adapt to night-vision goggles; we did survival drills and other scenarios we might encounter in the Middle East. All of these drills were done wearing full tactical vests loaded with multiple magazines, medical kit, flashlight, and knife. We had battle drills and classroom work to drive it all home—the way it would work in real life.

I wore that heavy battle vest all day long, even at lunch and on break. By the end of the day, I was covered in sweat, but I got used to the vest, to the point where it became second nature. Almost, anyway. That thing was heavy.

In one drill, we had to jump into the deep end of a pool, and the weight of the vest sent us right to the bottom, where we sat until we instinctively learned where the rip cord to release the vest was. I learned quickly, believe me.

Leo dropped me, my seabag, a laptop, and another duffel at San Diego International for the flight to Dulles, outside Washington, where a twelve-hour connecting flight to Kuwait awaited. The travel gods were with me. No screaming children, no crammed seating, just some breathing room, movies to watch, and XM radio to listen to, which made the flight seem bearable. On the flight to Kuwait, I saw three other of my colleagues, and when we landed, we all cleared customs together and headed for the stunning luxury of the Hilton Kuwait Resort.

And so much for the usual stories of the lonely soldier soldiering on as she accustoms herself to the deprivations of the war zone. While I shook off the jet lag after the long flight from Dulles, I suffered through the luxury of the Hilton, had a great meal, hit the gym, sent emails to Leo and my father, and generally soaked up the amenities.

While we waited to get into Iraq, I had the opportunity to get into the city, and for the first time in my life, an odd thing struck me: I was now a foreigner. It gave me a perspective that hung with me for my entire six months of my tour—and for my other overseas tours as well for that matter. It wasn't uncomfortable, just an odd perspective for a young woman who until a few years before had never really seen much beyond Ohio. But it was a positive, mindful perspective that would serve me well later, when I was interrogating prisoners and making decisions on their fates.

In those first days in Kuwait, I wondered—as I would later, in the house of the suspected Iraqi terrorist—what the Kuwaiti's thought of me. Especially the women, some of whom were dressed in the traditional Muslim purdah, which covered them completely.

As my NCIS career progressed, I realized in many ways I was a foreigner of sorts in my own office. That same feeling of apartness, of being different and slightly uncomfortable, would return to me. I was a woman in an office full of men for the most part. I was young in a work environment where many of my colleagues were seasoned veterans. I was a civilian in a bureaucracy world of ex-military guys. And I was a woman of color in a very white world. I would later learn that investigating gruesome suicides and sorting out terrorists would be far more palatable than working in an office with some of my colleagues.

On the day I headed to Al Asad, I took the last hot and comforting bath I'd have for six months and left the Hilton at 4:30 that morning. One thing I can assure you, and as anyone who knows me will tell you, I'm not a morning person. For the drive out to the Kuwait airport, I sat in the front seat with a colleague who was also heading into Iraq. I paid the price for my sleepiness. He talked my head off for the entire hour-long drive, enough to spark not-so-pleasant memories of my trips to Pittsburgh with my old boss, Daniel. I wished at one point I had had the foresight to jump in the back seat. But now, a year removed from the Pittsburgh trip, I was heading to Ali Al Salem Air Base in Kuwait City and then to my home for the next six months, Al Asad.

I guess that was a fair exchange.

My assignment in Al Asad, in the simplest of terms, called for me to lead a team of NCIS investigators charged with making decisions on the front line of the war against terrorism. In the political chaos of post-Saddam, postinvasion Iraq, in 2008, uncertainty was the rule, not the exception. And between the internal fighting for power and the external threats being thrown at US forces everywhere, there were many people in Iraq who might not have belonged where they were.

It would be our job to find out as much as we could about these people—a clue, perhaps, that might lead to Osama bin Laden. By tracking, or backtracking, the trail of a suspect picked up for laying IEDs in a roadbed and brought in for questioning, I might uncover a clue that could help find bin Laden.

Say for example that someone had been picked up because he had been seen acting suspiciously around a spot where an IED had later been found. And say that guy didn't have the proper identification or had an identification that was dubious. And say that during routine questioning, it became clear he was not an Iraqi—that maybe he spoke Arabic with a Yemeni accent, or maybe a Saudi one. It was our job with NCIS to see how much we could learn. It was pretty heady stuff, and I was more than prepared to do my part.

My destination was officially known as the Joint Prosecution and Exploitation Center. Our goal: to identify and neutralize foreign intelligence and possible international terrorists. In Iraq, for example, NCIS established a fingerprint lab in Fallujah to help identify insurgent operatives. Evidence collected after safe house raids, sniper incidents, and bombings was processed forensically. NCIS personnel operating with Marines at the Joint Prosecution and Exploitation Center used this and other evidence to identify and arrest hundreds of insurgents and build cases for their prosecution in Iraqi courts.

Once there, I would be in charge of managing a team of six—including Marines, sailors, and two interpreters. It was a mix of civilian and military that did not necessarily blend easily at times.

We prepared prosecutorial packages on all detainees captured. These packages would include any information we could find on the detainee, including any intelligence and criminal history—all from classified and unclassified systems. Based on what we could find out, I would recommend whether to keep or release the detainee and to send him off to more secure locations for further questioning.

I arrived in Iraq at the end of 2007, the year that President George W. Bush announced would be the year of what became known as "the Surge," where an additional two hundred thousand troops were sent in "to help Iraqis clear and secure neighborhoods, to help them protect the local population, and to help ensure that the Iraqi forces left behind are capable of providing the security."

Such a surge, the president said, would provide the time and conditions conducive to reconciliation among political and ethnic factions.

My first tour there was bookended by two events I wrote of earlier: In January, in the worst attack in Iraq in months, a suicide bomber killed thirty people at a home where mourners were paying their respects to the family of a man killed in a car bomb. When I left in June, at least sixty people were killed and about seventy-five wounded when an explosive-laden minibus exploded at a bus terminal near a crowded market in a Shiite district of Baghdad. The blast caused an apartment building to burst into flames. The US military attributed the bombing to a Shiite militia leader, Haydar Mehdi Khadum al-Fawadi, saying he orchestrated the bombing to incite sectarian violence between Sunnis and Shiites, the predominant Muslim sects in Iraq.

In October 2007, just two months before I arrived, and after almost a year of silence, Osama bin Laden issued a tape-recorded "Message to the People of Iraq," his third recorded speech in less than two months. In it, he described the situation in Iraq as "dire." Bin Laden was clearly talking about squabbling Iraqi factions previously loyal to Al Qaeda defecting to the new Iraqi government and Coalition forces various, which in reality really meant American troops.

"Some of you have been lax in one duty, which is to unite your ranks," bin Laden said. "Beware of division…Muslims are waiting for you to gather under a single banner to champion righteousness. Be keen to oblige with this duty."

This was the Iraq I was entering.

Home to the Second Marine Expeditionary Force, Al Asad Air Base was the second largest US military base in Iraq when I arrived. It sat in the largely Sunni western province of Al Anbar, about one hundred miles west of Baghdad. Al Asad became the largest Coalition base in western Iraq and the western equivalent of Baghdad's Green Zone.

A major convoy hub, it hosted hundreds of fuel and supply trucks every day, trucks whose noises I would quickly get used to. Huge shipments of fuel were commonly run along the dangerous routes coming out of Jordan in the days of the Surge, and despite insurgent attempts, a majority of these convoys arrived at their destinations untouched.

Al Asad was huge and offered amenities that included an indoor swimming pool, a movie theater, a post office, an enormous recreation center, several gyms, and a PX.

Lest anyone get too homesick, people on the base could choose to dine, if that's the proper word for it, at Burger King, Kentucky Fried Chicken, Pizza Hut, Subway, Cinnabon, or a Green Beans Coffee Shop.

And let me tell you, after the regular base chow, something from any of those places seemed like dining at a five-star restaurant.

Most of the housing on the base was called "cans"—shipping containers converted into living quarters, though there were some actual barracks. And in a crunch, with transient troops seeming to overflow the housing, base official set up tents for temporary quarters.

We would get, on occasion, indirect fire from Iraqi insurgents that never really caused much damage. I was never worried when I was there about that.

When we finally reached the base for the first time after our flight from Kuwait, our new hosts ran us ragged with what seemed to me a bit of an overdone and hectic tour of everything. I mean, I was tired to begin with. It had been a long trip from San Diego, and the brief respite at the Kuwait Hilton hadn't fully recharged me.

In quick order, we visited the post office, the NCIS office, the chow hall, and a gym. After being shown my temporary quarters, I forced myself to have a workout at the gym, then later had my first meal on base. It was fairly decent, I have to say, but it was a long shot from the king crab I had had with Leo only a few days earlier.

When I awoke that first morning, I was exhausted, which I guess is not surprising. But I found it difficult to sleep because I was so excited about what the next six months would bring, about my first interrogation, and about my place in the War on Terror.

I resisted the urge to head for the bathroom in the early-morning darkness, though. One of the tidbits I'd picked up on our whirlwind tour of the base the day before was a story about the huge and ugly camel spiders that like to surprise early-morning visitors to the head.

But with the first light, I jumped up and began a morning routine that I'd follow every day I was at the base for the next six months. I quickly adapted— it really only took a few days—to the night noises of the constant fuel convoys and the landings and takeoffs of planes. Then I quickly mastered the art of the four-minute shower in brownish-orange water that can do some serious damage to hair and skin if you don't let it run and clear for a bit. I'd follow that with a half-decent breakfast. Once I got used to the powdered eggs.

Shortly after I settled in, I tried to call Leo back at our house in San Diego to see how he was adapting to his new Robyn-less routine. We were disconnected. I should have taken that as some sort of symbolic sign. When I later caught up with him by email, I learned that he had somehow "accidentally" withdrawn too much money from our joint account. What he spent it on, he didn't say, but he did write that he was having problems paying a few bills.

Not a good sign, but what could I do?

But things soon drifted into a welcoming routine, and when you're far from home in the middle of the Iraqi desert, routine is welcome. I worked my cases, went to the "gym," and settled in.

I quickly learned that close quarters can prove testing at times. I was working a case one afternoon in the NCIS office a few weeks after I arrived while one of my colleagues blasted heavy metal so loudly I felt the beginnings of a headache. I assumed he had not yet heard of headphones.

But this is the type of situation in close quarters where you just have to grin and bear it. If I complained, things would have become very tense, very quickly.

And there was nowhere to go. Grudges, resentments, petty politics all became more acute there.

I also got my first taste of the cultural gulf between Americans and our Iraqi interpreters, and how small misunderstandings can transcend language. Nina, one of our interpreters, people who were absolutely vital to our mission, grabbed and sat in my colleague May's chair, which May thought was both mean and disrespectful. It seemed a simple misunderstanding, but it ran deeper than that, and it made me more aware of subtleties that ruled our existence there. Earlier in an interrogation, May felt Nina had translated the word "black" into something in Arabic that more closely resembled "slave man." May took it as an insult and had been angry since. The chair incident only brought things to a head. Lesson? All things are not always what they appear to be.

By the end of February, I had settled in and had begun analyzing intelligence from various sources, sorting through reports, interrogating suspects, and making recommendations to either let someone go or send them off for further questioning at a more secure area.

And that's when I had my worst day of the tour, February 28, 2008. It was a day I had done everything to avoid, what I had worked so hard against. I was dumped from a mission because I was a woman.

I had done everything I thought I needed to do to make the men accept me as an equal. It was men, after all, who ruled the base, who were the macho leaders and role models for everyone else. Women, I learned, regardless of training or inclination or experience, were meant to be protected. I'm not sure if it was simply an age-old instinct among the guys or just an unpleasant offshoot of men in the military.

Regardless, I was a woman in a man's world and a civilian to boot. This was a world where everything, from where you could live to how you addressed someone to even where you could unwind after work, was governed by rank and customs and military order.

When I went to bed the night before, I had been part of a "fly away team," a group that would head off base to investigate a suspicious homicide with Iraqi police.

The next morning I was awakened around 6:30 by a commotion outside, three guys arguing loudly about something. By 7:30, I was up and in my flight suit, ready to hop on a helicopter to head to the investigation site in what was most likely hostile territory—not an unusual situation since almost everywhere outside the base was hostile territory.

But I had been excited about the prospect and ready for it. It would have been a great learning experience for me, and the Iraqis wanted NCIS there to watch and advise.

That's why I was in Iraq, after all.

After breakfast, I returned to my room to get a few last-minute items, when one of the mission coordinators knocked to tell me the rest of the mission had started without me. They just took off and didn't tell me.

The night before we had all talked about the day's plans and what I would do. To learn that the team had left without me, that they didn't have the nerve to even tell me but simply took off, was at first hurtful, like I just took a sharp knife to the back.

It was my worst nightmare.

Then I became angry. I had finally had a chance to put all my training and experience into something, and I was essentially kicked to the curb because I was a woman.

Later, apologies flowed, but the same thing continued—the same undercurrents of "women can't cut it" were never far from the surface.

I quickly came to the conclusion that I loved the work and was energized by it. I felt I was part of a group with an admirable goal—keeping track of terrorists. The job was fine; it was certain people who made things difficult.

Later, another incident only reinforced that thought. I quickly learned we did not live or work in a world where people had work lives and private lives, where they worked one place, then went home to another. In a situation like Al Asad, work, personal, and recreational time was all intermingled. You couldn't get away from it or from people who might cause some friction. On top of that, throw in the fact that we were trapped in an environment where outside sat any number of people who would love to kill you. That was volatile.

One example of this was an incident that took place before one of our team members, Ken, was shipping out and a number of us on the NCIS team were jockeying to take over his lead investigator position. For me, it seemed another step up, a job with more responsibility.

Enter Rich, a guy with just the kind of personality that spells out Bad Chemistry. Rich was a self-appointed guru of all things, and he took it on himself to tell others on the team that I wasn't equipped to take over Ken's job, that I would not be a good match. I was a woman, he said, and would be easily intimidated.

When I confronted him about this campaign of his, he denied ever saying a thing. I wondered whether I was still back in high school in Cincinnati.

Mingled with the tensions of working in Iraq, with the suicide bombers and the unrest and the work to make the proper reports, feeling constantly that I held someone's very existence in my hands—to set them free or send them to jail—I prayed daily to be able to make the right decisions.

But life happens, no matter where you are.

Leo was in San Diego, holding down the fort. And even though he was living in my house for free, and driving my car, and using a joint bank account funded almost entirely by me, I had a deep appreciation for him and what he was doing.

But he was in San Diego, and I was in Iraq. And in the close quarters of Al Asad, despite my best intentions, I was falling in love.

I had met Nate, a fellow NCIS investigator. We shared a love for working out, a calmness under fire, and a love for our work. Nate had a great sense of humor and an impressive attitude. We grew closer each day, despite my inclinations to stay away from what could only be trouble.

Trying to make a decision tore me up.

The fact that I later learned Leo was cheating on me almost from the day I left, and had been helping himself to liberal chunks of my money, did provide some solace later. But while I was in Iraq and falling for Nate, I struggled to find the right answer and had many sleepless nights deciding what to do and whom to choose.

It wasn't easy; Nate had been married before and had a young son, and becoming an instant mother did not have a great amount of appeal to me. But I fell for Nate pretty hard. He left Iraq before I did, to China Lake, and begged me to join him.

I was torn up.

That soap opera aside, I lived for missions off the base, for the chance to see something other than the camp and to feel, actually feel, I was in a foreign country doing dangerous and important work.

In a war zone, things don't always work on schedule, and often missions planned well ahead of time might be bounced because of a sandstorm, or because a colonel has diverted a plane we planned to use. Working there meant getting used to a lot of false alarms, a lot of waiting, and at times boredom.

And the accommodations outside at what were termed "forward operating bases" could sometimes border on the just plain weird—sometimes nothing more than a box with a bed inside.

But these outside trips were fairly often a mix of obstacles, danger, and things so common you would think you were at the beach: a rugged, bouncing, jarring convoy trek out to a jobsite; armed guards while we worked; and then an evening grilling burgers and hot dogs. Grill the suspects, grill the burgers, I guess you could say.

I did see some things that made me wonder how things would be when the American forces left. Some of the Iraqi forces at our jobs off the base looked to be no more than teenagers. And they appeared to be uninterested in what was going on. What will happen when they don't have to answer to American commanders? I thought. Was what we were doing there worth the effort and the lives lost?

These outside trips also brought adventures to personal hygiene not seen outside the United States. I learned, among other specialties, how to "shower" with body wipes and water bottles, and how to use a "wag" bag, a sort of outhouse in a Ziploc bag arrangement. Nice.

And more often than not, "interviews" produced nothing. But I still enjoyed them because they gave me a chance to see Iraq from the ground, and foot patrols gave me the opportunity to talk to the Marines who always provided our security. I was always impressed with them, and I always felt safe.

As my tour wound down, I had one last memorable foot patrol, to Rawah, to a skilled craftsman's shop owned by an Iraqi who had been very useful in providing us with information and pointing us in most cases to productive finds and people.

This, to me, was what I had really come to Iraq for.

It was an edgy trip into Rawah, though, as these trips can get when the team is not working together or is off-balance a bit. My colleague Jeff was on edge the entire time, snippy and jumpy and not acting himself. I had to remind him several times about procedures, and he snapped back at me to mind my own business. I wonder if he had been reprimanded for something.

When we got to the craftsman's shop, though, Jeff's overbearing and anxious tone with the Iraqis we had come to see led me to know instantly we were going nowhere with the visit. It's amazing how in any language and with any culture, being obnoxious translates to the same thing. You annoy people and you put them off.

Al Asad Range Day on January 6, 2008. I am in the middle.

In front of MRAP somewhere in Iraq on March 14, 2008.

My Last Day in Al Asad, Iraq, on June 15, 2008.

Four

THE COLONEL

My time in Iraq also introduced me to what at first was a minor irritation, something I could easily push to the side. But it became much later an ugly specter and daily reminder that would by the end leave me unable to breathe, to concentrate, to live with the normal joy I applied to everything. It seemed so minor at the time. But as I would learn later, it is a very real problem that affects thousands of women in the workplace every day and has resulted in millions of dollars in lost work time and lawsuits that have cost companies far more than dollars.

Two months into my time at Al Asad, I got the very first inkling that I had somehow stepped back in time to an era when a woman was expected to be silent, to have children and take care of her man and never question any-thing—especially a man's wisdom and experience and, well, manhood.

Far back in my mind, far enough to allow me to give them only passing and brief thought, the questions started creeping in. Did the über-macho at-mosphere that saturated NCIS bring this out in men who would otherwise have gotten in step with the twenty-first century—or at least pretended to? Were these the sort of guys who were hired, most likely, by other guys who thought the same way?

At the time, I had been flush with the true joy of doing something so de-manding and at times so stressful it didn't seem worth even a second thought. I was a lead investigator on the front edge of the war against terrorism. I was getting favorable reviews, and I felt I was making a big difference. So what if a bunch of lunkheaded men whose attitudes about women had not changed since maybe the turn of the century—that is, the turn of the last century, say around 1910—when women are only good "barefoot and pregnant" and considered the weaker sex.

Add to the already high-testosterone atmosphere of NCIS the similar—perhaps even greater—machismo of the military, the Marines even, and most people would be able to get the picture of at least the potential for male-female conflict.

But I didn't. I was on too much of a high, too much of a roll. I would later, of course, but at the time, I just wrote it off.

There is a great line from a Bob Seger song I think of these days: "I wish I didn't know now what I didn't know then." That about sums it up.

My first inkling was sparked after an American was killed off base in a friendly fire incident, shot in the dark after his patrol wandered into a zone they weren't supposed to wander into. Even though this was not our primary mission, it was still a death under circumstances that required an explanation. It would have been one of my first chances to go outside and to watch and learn the painstaking way such an investigation is undertaken. Years later in Afghanistan, I had not only mastered these techniques, I was praised for my investigative abilities. But that was later.

At the time, I was still relatively new and fresh. And as it turns out, I was also a woman. Even though I had been scheduled to leave on a morning helicopter to the scene with two of my male colleagues, they left without me.

I later learned that one of the men involved had serious issues with women in law enforcement. I was truly and engagingly pissed off. And I made my point clear when they returned. The issue had absolutely nothing to do with my lack of experience and everything to do with my being a woman.

They would not have left a new *guy* behind. I don't want to make assumptions, but I am positive they would have just let him go on the mission and watch and learn things for himself. I think my age and gender played into much of what my male cohorts thought I could and couldn't do. I don't think they particularly enjoyed the fact that I was in such a position of responsibility and young and a woman—it was almost too much for them.

The agent responsible for the decision to leave me behind later apologized for what he himself admitted was his "arrogance." But I later learned that even after that apology to me, he continued to talk about my lack of ability behind my back. I believe the term for that is "insincere."

Part of our job on the criminal investigative side was interrogating detainees—and I say "our" because at the time I had been invigorated by the sense of camaraderie and teamwork. We would normally interrogate in pairs, working with detainees in a sort of good cop/bad cop routine. Male agents seemed to need to dominate the interrogation, which I think was an ego thing. The same agent who left me behind on the death investigation loved dominating interrogations, and my own thoughts were to simply let him. I didn't feel the need to push it and simply let him. As a result, I usually played the good cop role in the interrogations. I also knew and understood that Middle Eastern men did not respect women, and by deferring to a male colleague, I was aware we would in the end have a more successful session.

These sensibilities on my part, however, were construed as a sign of weakness, of an unwillingness on my part to be aggressive.

But the truly single most prolific practitioner of the male-dominance theory was a Marine Corps lieutenant colonel I will simply refer to as the Colonel.

NCIS, despite its apparent connection with the Navy, is a civilian organization, and its investigators and support personal are mostly civilian. In Iraq, we were charged with, among other things, investigating and preparing the prosecutorial packages against the detainees. Because these detainees were more often than not captured by the military, our office was supervised by Marines—initially a master sergeant and then later the Colonel. Since everything in any government situation demands a rank of some sort to determine who has more clout (and I guess also to determine who makes more money), NCIS investigators were determined to hold the same rank as a military officer.

But the whole civilian versus military way of doing things was never a smooth and efficient blend of strengths. The military almost demands a hierarchy to work. And in our situation, the military guys automatically assumed we were their subordinates, which was not the case. I don't think anyone ever truly understood the various roles—especially the Colonel, a Marine career officer whose sensibilities and sensitivities were, shall I say, not apparent.

Interestingly, I found the young enlisted Marines who would from time to time serve as NCIS escorts off base to be far more enlightened and oblivious to the normal colorations of rank and privilege. One young Marine once told me on patrol, "They have the rank, but God blessed me with the brains." I felt that was exactly the case: those with rank tried to test their rank and throw their ranks at me. But it didn't work. I was civilian, and they had no authority over me, which was hard for the officers to understand. The younger Marines were not as corrupted and in many aspects in my same generation; we just understood each other.

When the Colonel arrived, I honestly think that, in order of confusion, he was perplexed first about women being in positions of authority and leadership and second about civilians in general. He had been in the military far too long and seemed to view civilians and life outside the Marine Corps as some sort of alien existence—as if we were Martians invading his space.

He struggled with the relationship as a whole, and having been in leadership positions for so long and having so many people instinctively do as he said when he said it, he was ultimately shocked when NCIS agents challenged him. That would have been unheard of at Camp Lejeune, his most recent assignment before he came to Iraq, where he was in charge of an entire operation. And the oil in the frying pan was heated up even more so because this was his last assignment before retiring, and I believe he was not about to go out with a whimper, cowing to civilians' demands and lack of respect. To say nothing, of course, about the fact that one of those civilians was me, a woman, and a young woman to boot. The military has always and traditionally looked at women as the weaker sex; men and women coexist in a community because society says they have to. The military has always viewed men as beacons of strength and women as weak. In many cases, military men don't like to have women around because they feel women get special privileges. Combine that with the fact that most in the military feel that civilians can get away with things because we are free birds. See what I mean? I was about to step into a perfect storm.

As you can imagine, trying to work with the Colonel was perfect hell. He would order, and I would gently explain we couldn't. No matter how many times I explained to him as a lead investigator what I could and could not do, the legal intricacies just didn't sink in. Our responsibilities were tightly controlled, and he simply did not grasp that. It was almost as if he were so stupefied by my failing to carry out his orders quickly and efficiently that he simply could not act.

I know that the Colonel sought almost from our first meeting to have me replaced with a male, because another male colleague told me. And I know also that when we first began interacting, the Colonel would ask questions of male NCIS agents first before coming to me.

The Colonel's inability to accept a female in a position of authority was made clear to me almost from the start when he ordered a man to accompany me on a short mission outside the base—something I had been doing for some time quite efficiently by myself. I wasn't sure if he felt I needed protection or guidance, some sort of big brother to make sure I was safe. But I was insulted.

One morning, after I had braided my hair in an authentic African style, he called me into his office, asked me what was wrong with it, and demanded to know if NCIS allowed such things. I told him it was a style worn frequently by people of African descent, which seemed to confuse him. To me, it was a display of his shallowness and lack of culture. I did not respond with anger but rather with an attempt to open his eyes to cultural differences. But the whole odd scene solidified my thoughts about his total separation from normal life outside the Marine Corps.

Later, in what I think was simply a misguided effort to assert his authority, he banned a weekly poker night NCIS investigators had been doing for months with the master sergeant, saying he felt gambling was inappropriate. We didn't even play for money, and the poker night was nothing more than a morale-building team night sort of thing. Our backlash was an immediate and vocal no. It was these sorts of small game-playing, power-testing forays by that colonel that made working for him all the more stressful, which of course was totally unnecessary.

He went out of his way to find fault with things I did, which was blatantly clear to the others. Once, he spent more than an hour looking for me because he needed to have three numbers on a report I had written for him changed. I changed them and said nothing. He won. But the fact is, he wasted an hour to show his authority, and I made the changes in literally ten seconds. Was that efficient?

On a number of occasions, almost in a petulant "because I can, that's why" snit, he would order me to reinterrogate detainees and modify reports—once after I had spent several hours doing so and was about to release the prisoner. There was no reason to do so; there was clearly no evidence against this particular man, but the Colonel insisted because the Colonel could.

The Colonel did not do that with any of my male colleagues. He did not ignore the advice of other male agents; in fact, he often sought advice. It was almost as if he were genetically incapable of accepting women in any way or form as equals.

At the time, I thought it was just him. I would later learn that was not the case, much to my dismay.

Disarmed

9 June 2008

Dear Ms. Robyn S. Coleman,

I would like to take this opportunity to offer you my sincere thanks and appreciation for a job well done during your tour with the Naval Criminal Investigative Service Resident Agency (NCISRA), Camp Fallujah, Multinational Force - West. Your personal contribution as well as the contribution of your agency, has made a significant, positive, and lasting impact on our efforts toward maintaining the operational readiness of our combat forces as we push toward establishing the rule of law and provincial Iraqi control in Al Anbar Province.

NCISRA Iraq is dedicated to investigating and mitigating criminal, terrorist and intelligence threats affecting the Marine Corps and Navy personnel, as well as all Coalition Forces. The quick response, resolution, and thoroughness of your investigations and operations have assisted in deterring future criminal activity, thus allowing the men and women serving in Multinational Force – West to effectively and efficiently carry out their duties. Further your efforts at NCISRA Iraq Camp Fallujah directly support our overall mission of enabling Al Anbar Province to be a productive partner in a peaceful and federal Iraq.

Despite the personal hardship of a deployment away from your family and friends, you volunteered to support Multinational Force – West and I commend you for your high degree of esprit, hard work and dedication to the mission throughout your tour. Your professional contribution in support of I Marine Expeditionary Forces (Forward) has made a difference and is indicative of the superb quality of support provided by NCIS to Multinational Force – West and the Marine Corps. Job well done Robyn.

Semper Fidelis,

JOHN F. KELLY
Major General, U.S. Marine Corps
Commanding General
I Marine Expeditionary Force (Forward)

A write-up from Major General Kelly on June 9, 2008.

Five

DJIBOUTI

After Al Asad, I considered myself a veteran who had seen it all—bombs, mayhem, death, danger, and internal bickering—all wrapped in the deflating odor of sexual harassment. At least that is what I was thinking as the plane lifted off for my trip back to Kuwait and eventually on home to San Diego. At the time, I might have thought of myself as a veteran, but not too many of my male colleagues did.

I had a friend, an acquaintance, actually. He was a friend of a friend, and he'd grown up on a farm and was constantly teased about his lack of sophistication—and he really was naive about many things. But I think that was an endearing trait. He looked for the best in many things. But he wasn't a head-in-the-clouds type of guy. One of his trademarks was saying "I didn't just fall off the hay wagon." He knew what was going on. He knew life was complicated and at times ugly. He just preferred to look at the better sides of things. He was an optimist.

Well, I hadn't just fallen off the hay wagon either. I had known there would be complications being a young woman in a world full of macho guys—ex-military macho guys, to be more specific. So I essentially wrote off my own seeming inability to rise above the fray, as it were. So what if my male colleagues saw me as a woman first, a young woman second, and a very competent investigator third? After Al Asad, I felt that I'd just give them the benefit of the doubt. After all, I was in many ways a rookie. This was my first time out and my first time getting involved with some at times very messy investigations. It will get easier the more experience I pile up, I'd tell myself.

49

Then I might be seen as "one of the guys." Too bad that was an aspiration—to be one of the guys. Why couldn't I have simply been one of the NCIS crew?

I put all those thoughts aside on the plane back home. I had done a great job over there and seen a lot. It was time to regroup and enjoy some serenity. I deserved a little break and had earned some peace and quiet and reenergizing.

But what I was met with ended up being far from blissful and calm. My life was about to undergo some major changes, including an engagement to Nate, some decompression time in Georgia, more of my magic-touch networking to get away from San Diego, and the volatility that was Jane, my supervisor. Despite the danger of Iraq and its complicated sexual politics, I almost felt I'd rather stay there than work for Jane again.

In the interest of fairness, I do have to point to a reaffirming event that showed men and women colleagues could be friends and enjoy the normal things friends do to help each other. As strained as the male-female chemistry in Al Asad was—especially with the Colonel and the men of the military when it came to professional, work-related interactions—I would be unfair to paint all the men at Al Asad with the same broad brush.

I made friends with men there, and we had normal interactions without the sexual tension. One of these guys was Mark, who flew back to the States with me after our tour in Al Asad ended. Before I left Al Asad, I had plotted with Mark's wife, Nicole, through emails to plan a surprise for him when we got back, and surprise him we did.

While Mark and I, fresh off the plane, went out for our first real, non-chow-line meal at a PF Chang's in Jacksonville, Florida, Nicole waited in the restaurant parking lot. A very tired, very hungry, very jet-lagged Mark nearly had a major coronary when Nicole walked up to our table dressed to impress. I could see the shock and utter confusion, but extreme lust and love, of seeing his wife right there before him. It was a wonderful moment, arranged for a friend by a friend and his wife. That's how it should have been all the time.

▲ ▲ ▲

When I stepped off the plane with Mark after Al Asad, I didn't realize the next months would be interesting, exciting, and crazy. And looking back at it now, I realize they would bring me closer to my Cincinnati dreams of seeing the world, working an exciting and meaningful job, and truly getting to know another culture and country.

But that was after a six-month bicoastal whirlwind of moves and long drives and blissful vacations after I returned to the States.

By February 2009, I was headed out again, to Africa, to Camp Lemonnier, in Djibouti, nestled in the famous Horn of Africa and centered in a politically explosive and strategically vital area. From the day I stepped off the plane in African heat and humidity until the day I left four months later, Djibouti was an experience that helped me grow more than any other of my NCIS assignments. I loved nearly every minute of the professional challenges and the scents and sweetness and rhythms of Djibouti.

In Iraq, as I would learn later in Afghanistan, Americans live in self-imposed, self-created vacuums. Granted, we were in war zones, and it was necessary for protection. But the almost stunning ability to create Little Americas in the middle of the Iraqi desert, complete with fast-food restaurants, movie theaters, gyms—all the comforts of home—spoke to me of an unhealthy isolation. It was possible for Americans serving in those places to never once speak to an Iraqi, taste Iraqi food, or get even the slightest glimpse of Iraqi culture. I know, it was a war zone, but not everyone was trying to kill us. I often wonder if that complete isolation, that total separation from a group of people we were ostensibly trying to save, in the end widen a gap that should have and easily could have been closed. We were helping them; we were lifting bonds of terror that many lived with for decades under Saddam Hussein—and we were willing to die to do so. We should have been welcomed with open arms, protected. But instead we stayed isolated and mistrusted. And I think some of the people I worked with in Iraq could have just as easily spent six months in the middle of the desert in Utah for all they learned about Iraq.

That's why my tour in Djibouti was refreshing. It is unfortunate that the simple mention of Djibouti and Camp Lemonnier now brings with it an almost paralyzing darkness—a nightmarish haze I want to avoid. But that would come later, after my second tour there. The first tour was a lesson in how things could and should work.

The fact that I could get out and off the base at Camp Lemonnier, that I could mingle and learn rather than be protected and feared as I was as an American in Iraq, had a great deal to do with the invigorating and energizing African experience.

And did I mention pirates?

I suspect that also had something to do with adding some high voltage to the assignment. I was chosen to be part of a team of NCIS investigators from a number of countries that was the first on the scene following an ill-fated pirate attack on an American-flagged ship, the *Maersk Alabama*, in the Gulf of Aden. Modern-day pirates, violent, well practiced, unforgiving, and in many ways ingenious, had long plagued shipping in the waters off the Horn of Africa. Armed pirates, efficient and aggressive, could board a tanker in minutes from fast small boats and hold a crew and its cargo hostage under the very real threat of death. It was a frequent and all-too-common occurrence that ships with valuable cargoes passing through the Gulf could do little about, it seemed. Owners considered getting through the Gulf safely a victory of sorts. Losing a cargo without loss of life was a more hollow victory but acceptable. But piracy and its attendant damages was simply added to the debit side of the ledger as a cost of doing business in the profitable exchanges of world trade in that area. While the outcome of the *Maersk Alabama* incident was deemed a triumph for America, officials in many countries plagued by pirates said it was not likely to discourage piracy in general. Shortly after the *Maersk Alabama* incident, a report noted that pirates were still holding a dozen ships with more than two hundred crew members and millions of dollars of cargo.

But the pirates who hit the *Maersk Alabama* made a mistake. And they paid for it with their lives after a dramatic five-day standoff that ended with snipers and Navy SEALs. And I was one of the first investigators on the scene, chosen to be a member of the NCIS team that began the April 2009 investigation.

A year later, the man recognized as the leader of the pirates, Abduwali Abdukhadir Muse, pleaded guilty in a New York City court to charges that included seizing a ship by force, hostage taking, and kidnapping, among others. US Attorney Preet Bharara, who led the prosecution team, said after the guilty plea that he wanted to "make clear that modern-day piracy is a crime against the international community and a form of terrorism on the high seas. Pirates who attack U.S. ships overseas and take American hostages should know that they will face stiff justice in an American courtroom. I would like to recognize the extraordinary collective efforts of local, federal, and international law enforcement and pay special thanks to the men and women of the U.S. Navy without whose bravery today's result would not have been possible."

He added another reference to us specifically, thanking "the Naval Criminal Investigative Service for their extraordinary efforts in the investigation of this case."

Three years after the incident and our role in it, outgoing NCIS director Thomas Betro was still talking about it and pointing to it as a glowing example of how NCIS works:

> We played a major role in collecting intelligence against pirates, investigating acts of piracy, and supporting prosecutions of pirates. Special agents work aboard U.S. Navy ships that are tasked with defending the shipping and the maritime industry against pirates.
>
> With *Maersk Alabama* specifically, we went to the crime scene of the lifeboat where Captain Phillips was held and the pirates were subdued. We did a full crime-scene investigation and gathered evidence to support prosecution—forensics, interviews, and interrogations. We also had to assist in determining legal jurisdiction—where would a case be prosecuted? Many factors were considered, but the surviving pirate, Abduwali Muse, was ultimately brought to New York for prosecution.

Yeah, that was me.

It was heady stuff for us, and I was justifiably proud to be included as a part of it. Of course the Hollywooded-up Tom Hanks version of this whole intriguing incident, which came to the screen as *Captain Phillips* in 2013, was a bit different from the reality I was involved with in Mombasa, Kenya, in 2009. Then, I have to confess, it was just another challenging job for me to do. One thing the movie seemed to do was give much credit to the FBI in the investigation. But that's Hollywood for you.

But before I got to Mombasa for the *Maersk* investigation, before I even got to Djibouti, I had to decompress from Al Asad. You have to give credit to

NCIS for its consideration of employees and its ability to recognize that six months in a hostile Iraq environment can produce some stress-related problems that needed to be let out, that we had to settle back into the real world.

And that is precisely what I did, I think. Or at least what I tried to do. My decompression had some compression points of its own. I seem to get bored easily.

Here is what I did during what the NCIS terms an important transition period for people returning from the stress of a war zone: I networked with all the energy I had to make sure I got a transfer from the San Diego office and Jane. I cleaned up my house after kicking Leo out earlier for being a total slug, running up bills, cheating on me, and basically ruining my car. With the hardship bonus money I earned in Iraq, I supervised the installation of central air conditioning in my San Diego house.

I also began dating Nate, who was then stationed in nearby China Lake. Our attraction and love for each other managed to survive even in the tight quarters and tensions of Iraq. Free of those restrictions in California, the love that had started in the Iraqi desert blossomed big time. Our new courtship was invigorating and so different from our time in the pressure-cooker environment of Al Asad. We took a great and long Vegas vacation. I introduced Nate to my mother and sister while they were in San Diego visiting.

I wrangled an assignment at one of NCIS's chief hubs in Glynco, Georgia, where Nate had transferred later from China Lake. Nate and I got engaged at Thanksgiving, with him proposing to me at my parents' house in Cincinnati. I returned to San Diego and cleaned up the last of my cases there and bid a not-so-sad adieu to Jane.

Nate flew to California and helped me move to Glynco with a cross-country trip that we did almost nonstop in a day and a half. Let me tell you, that is some serious and tiring driving. It was not how I would have done it, believe me. I'm surprised Nate even allowed time for bathroom breaks. I'm sure if he could have rigged something up, we would have been peeing into bottles and eating cold sandwiches the entire way across the country. I have no idea what we saw or passed through. It was all highway all the time. We celebrated the record drive by spending our first Georgia night together in his cockroach-infested apartment.

How romantic.

In very short order, we then found and bought a house together.

That's how I spent my decompression time between deployments. So much for rest and relaxation.

I think I enjoyed it, though.

But the time in Georgia passed quickly and routinely, and my wanderlust and urge to get back into something more exotic soon began stirring. And when an opening came up for the Djibouti assignment, I bid on it, with Nate's blessing. And I got it.

So in February 2009, I was on my way overseas again—this time around to the rich and fabled Horn of Africa—to Djibouti, an impoverished former French colony with fewer than one million people, scarce natural resources, and what I would soon learn was fairly miserable hot weather.

But I loved it.

The legendary Horn of Africa lies along the southern side of the Gulf of Aden and is today as much of a political powder keg as it was when I arrived. It lies a relatively short distance from the part of the Arabian Peninsula considered the birth of Islam, an important consideration and what makes the Horn one of the most contentious regions of our contentious world. The Horn's proximity to the Arabian Peninsula meant that local merchants and sailors living on the Horn gradually came under the influence of the new religion through their Muslim trading partners

Each of the countries that comprise the Horn—Somalia, Ethiopia, Eritrea, Djibouti, and Sudan—suffers from serious internal and external political strife. And it's been that way for more than 150 years, first when the British Empire sought to control the Red Sea and later when Egypt tried to exert its power over the waters of the Nile and the extremely valuable Suez Canal.

Later, during the Cold War, the countries of the Horn became prized allies for their strategic locations. And over the years, each would routinely switch allegiance to principally the United States or the Russians as those world powers played an intricate and ever-changing game of political chess, both the American and the Russians each vying to win this at least temporary loyalty.

After 9/11, the value of the Horn became even more emphatic, and the struggle to control the countries of the Horn and establish their loyalty has become crucial on the Global War on Terror.

Considering the internal turbulence of the countries of the Horn and the decades-long conflicts and wars and enmities that still seethe close to the surface, I have to say that between Ethiopia, Somalia, Eritrea, and Djibouti, I was lucky to settle in the latter.

Djibouti was and is by far the most stable of the countries of the Horn, which of course was why the large American presence there was allowed.

Djibouti in general, and Camp Lemonnier specifically, my home for the next four months, was central to the prevailing strategy on the War on Terror. That meant drone aircraft, and plenty of them, sent on their robotic missions to Somalia and north across the Gulf of Aden to Yemen and beyond in the American mission to eliminate or at least disrupt Al Qaeda and Al Shabab.

That meant of course that Camp Lemonnier was an inviting target to any number of groups. For me, as part of the first line of defense there, that meant a very busy time sorting out real and imagined security threats.

American involvement with the sunbaked Camp Lemonnier—which was originally established by the French Foreign Legion in the early part of the last century—began with the base's use as a temporary staging area for US Marines. It quickly became an increasingly busy—and secret—base for Predator drones, the busiest outside Afghanistan at the time. Almost the entire five-hundred-acre base is dedicated to the Pentagon's War on Terror.

During my time at Lemonnier, there were I guess about three hundred special ops people dealing with the drone warfare campaign. But for me and my security work, the more important number was more than three thousand other troops, contractors, and civilians like me who were there to either train foreign militaries, gather intelligence, or dole out humanitarian aid across East Africa as part of a campaign to prevent extremists from taking root.

Among those troops was a stalker, who became the subject of one of my first investigations. While most of my work at Lemonnier dealt with security, both external and internal, I did have occasion to use my investigative skills on things at the base that had nothing to do with terrorism. One of my first cases was internal.

There is always tension, sexual and otherwise, in a camp where military men and women share confined areas and boredom. Many of the men and women on the base were restricted from traveling outside for obvious reasons.

Many were young and unsophisticated, thrown into the Global War on Terror right after they enlisted following high school graduation. For some, Djibouti was their first venture outside their hometown, let alone the country. These were not a group of people you let have free rein outside the control of their superiors, whether that was their platoon sergeant or their officers. Best to let them sit on base and be bored.

And for the most part, that's what they did. Boredom is safe.

But in one instance, the lack of something better to do led to an uncomfortable situation in which an enlisted female began seeing signs that someone had been watching her. He had left signs that he had been watching her as she went to the showers near her quarters, that he had been following her as she went to chow, and that he had been watching her prepare for sleep at night.

She filed a complaint, and I followed up, finding evidence that led quickly to a young noncom, who protested that his stalking was purely innocent. Innocent or not, I collected proof—cigarette butts outside her windows, comments to others, an online diary—enough to show that this had been going on longer than even the victim had thought. My job is and was to present findings, not to make recommendations or judgments. I presented the evidence I collected, and the man was relieved of his duties and sent home. For me, it was just another day's work.

Camp Lemonnier rolls across flat, sandy terrain on the edge of Djibouti City, which I soon learned was a sleepy city with sometimes weirdly empty streets.

Hemmed in by the sea and residential areas, Camp Lemonnier's primary shortcoming is that it has no space to expand. It is forced to share a single runway with Djibouti's only international airport, as well as an adjoining French military base and the tiny Djiboutian armed forces. Additionally, the base provides employment for approximately one hundred local and third-country-nation workers, a group that I came to rely on for my own work.

My journey to the Horn began with a difficult goodbye with Nate—the thought that I wouldn't see him for four months was almost wrenching.

I headed to Djibouti in early February 2009, coincidentally through Paris. Considering the enormous French influence in Djibouti, Paris was a very nice way to ease back into a foreign deployment.

Over the years, I've learned to develop a traveler's mind-set, to not expect or even want American amenities in places I've dropped into. Paris was a lesson in that exercise. I went through a range of opinions at first in Paris, probably because I was hungry and very tired when I landed. It's unfriendly, boring, and cold, I thought.

That was the reaction of a close-minded traveler and not something I ever wanted to classify myself as. Once I got some sleep and food, my next days in Paris, I found to my great delight, were wonderful. Parisians were actually friendly, the city was meant for walkers and bikers, not drivers, and I walked and shopped and ate and had a great time while I geared up for Africa. It was a terrific stop, and I'm glad I took the time to take a breath and see rather than just react.

The Parisian glow lasted just until I got on the plane to Djibouti. It seemed that every row had its own crying baby, and with a delayed takeoff, the good karma from my lark evaporated fairly quickly.

Such is travel in the fast lane to Africa, I guess.

That slightly ajar feeling, when you're not quite settled, when you're nervous about a new job in a new and different place, was amplified even more when I stepped off the plane in Djibouti. It is truly a third-world country, far more jarring than Iraq. At first tired glance, it seemed so impoverished, with plastic trash bags everywhere, and the people I saw walking so slowly along the roadway seeming so small and frail. I was overcome with sadness.

At first, Lemonnier didn't seem much better, a little shabby, a little worse for the wear. But I soon realized I would have everything I needed for the next four months, so why complain? I quickly found the gym—of course—the post office, the dining area, and the pool. My quarters were fine—not Hilton, Kuwait City, fine, but they'd work. Certainly better than the shipping crate I once slept in in Iraq.

My official title in Djibouti was lead special agent, and I would be conducting criminal investigations throughout the Horn. NCIS had teams in Kenya, Ethiopia, Djibouti, and Uganda, and we all worked closely together. And of course, for the *Maersk Alabama* case, I also worked with the FBI.

Create a small American base that is responsible for unleashing powerful and lethal attacks on suspected terrorist outposts, for sending out a steady stream of drones and planes capable of collecting intelligence not only in the region but on a much wider scale. Place it in the center of a volatile political region near the birthplace of Islam that has long been hostile to the West. Then demand that it be protected from all manner of threats, either real or perceived. There you would have Camp Lemonnier, Djibouti, and my job.

With the political volatility of the area, I kept very busy with investigations, many of them in some way related to the counterterrorist initiatives of the United States. And because of this, I ended up working closely with Djiboutian law enforcement officials as well.

I was busy from the start. Shortly after I arrived, the base received a threat, and I had to respond as the security officer—and I had to do that while a new lead broke in a terrorist investigation I was working on. Bingo. "Multitasking" took on new meaning at Lemonnier.

Some of the ongoing investigations called for working with Djiboutian law enforcement and also handling tensions on base created by feelings by Djiboutians who worked on the base that there seemed to be a double standard for rules governing behavior. Americans could get away with more—more noise, more curfew violations, more traffic infractions, and more public unruliness—than locals who worked there. The Americans and the Djiboutians seemed to almost enjoy harassing each other, and it often led to hard feelings if not fights. In fact, when I first began investigating the stalking incident, most Americans felt the culprit was undoubtedly a Djiboutian.

In addition to what seemed to me to be a never-ending number of cases, I was also the 24/7 duty agent. Sleep and relaxation quickly became something of a strange concept, something I would have to conjure up from my past.

Time passes quickly when you're busy, and time seemed to fly in Djibouti. There were a lot of high-adrenaline days that ended with a total exhausted collapse into bed. The next day, it would start all over again. I loved it.

My Djibouti tour was a far deeper immersion into a foreign culture than I had had in Iraq. I learned very quickly to look past the poverty and the shabbiness to find true beauty in a culture that was so much older and so much richer in many ways than our own.

In the grand scheme of things, especially in light of what would happen later during my next tour at Lemonnier, the most affirming, most strongly positive fact of my time there was how I worked with my supervisor. And how he worked with me. We complemented each other like perfectly synchronized gears, meshing silently and firmly as we went about our business. The key was mutual respect.

Algeron McCreary was an ideal supervisor—a man comfortable and confident in himself and in his abilities to lead. I often wonder if that is the key to what happened later. Al McCreary never felt threatened by me, never felt the need to undermine my work to make himself look better, never looked at me as a young woman he could take advantage of. He trusted me to do my job, and I did my job. It sounds so simple, but in practice, it proved in so many other of my assignments to be difficult if not impossible to pull off.

Al McCreary treated me with respect.

I couldn't help but contrast my work with Al with my times under Daniel in Cincinnati, Jane in San Diego, or the Colonel and others in Iraq. It continues to amaze me how the simple act of a manager telling you he knows you can do the job and do it well is so completely fulfilling. It seems that in so many managers respect is an alien concept. The managers, the bad ones, lead by edict, by bullying, by instilling fear—by asserting power when no such thing is needed.

I think that sort of dictatorial demeanor really has no place in an office.

Working with Al McCreary made my time in Djibouti professionally fulfilling. And the arrangement was reciprocal, as these things should be. I did everything I could to make him look good, to never have to explain any faults to his own supervisors.

It all seems so simple, yet such a thing seems so rare.

I soon settled into a rhythm that would govern my work for the next four months. I found the Djiboutians friendly and easy to work with, which made the open hostility I faced on the outside in Iraq seem so distant, like a bad dream.

And unlike Iraq, we could and did venture out. And I found that absorbing another culture, truly getting to understand it, was far more educational than I had imagined. My local forays were certainly far more educational than any of the indoctrination programs and seminars we absorbed on the base. It was real and visceral, not textbook. One of my first Djiboutian friends, a woman who helped me settle in and relax, was Fatima, a member of the Djiboutian gendarmerie. I was also helped a great deal by Charika, an interpreter from Eritrea, and Big Jo and Eli, who were almost always with us when we went off camp for various matters.

These two guys were the core of our office in my opinion, because without them we could not communicate with anyone, and without communication, we were useless—in a way deaf and blind to what was going on and to the cultural nuances that would have gone quickly over our heads.

Big Jo, a naturalized American citizen, was originally from Somalia. Eli had been born in Djibouti but was raised in the States.

Because of my friendships with Big Jo and Eli and others, I ate camel steak on a humid night in a local café where the diners were covered with flying bugs and lizards darted uninterrupted underfoot. On other occasions, I shared the delights of the spicy and flavorful Ethiopian food. I had delicious Ethiopian coffee prepared painstakingly and deliberately in a ritual ceremony that created an anticipation that made the dark and strong brew taste all that much better.

Imagine the concept of slowing down and living in the moment, of relishing the moment. Once I learned to enjoy that coffee ceremony, I could only think of the times I spent standing in line at Starbucks impatiently waiting for my grande latte.

In between the frenzy that work injected into my daily life, I did find time to speak with Nate as much as possible and to speak to my mother as we planned the wedding.

At times, I found Nate almost inflexible and unwilling to grasp the important concept that a couple needs to work together for a truly loving and understanding life together. Maybe it was just the difficulty of continuing a courtship through Skype and email and dealing with a time difference that brought differing moods at differing times. But there were times when I was perplexed about him and wondered if I really knew him despite our times together at Al Asad and in Georgia.

He sometimes became dramatic and emphatic about things that were important to me. Overly so, it seemed to me.

In one conversation, for example, he told me he didn't want me to hyphenate our married name, which I insisted on. My father had no boys, and

I wanted to carry on the Coleman name. What was so upsetting about that? And Nate didn't want my sister and I to get matching sister tattoos as we had long planned. And he didn't understand my braids and for that matter didn't make much of an effort to understand Black American culture. Which was weird, considering he was marrying me. If I hadn't mentioned it before, Nate is Italian.

But I was sure these were simply issues we would eventually resolve, and it didn't occupy too much of my time. Thank God I was so busy so often.

And as things do in close quarters, the sexual-tension issue and the harassment I had found so annoying at Al Asad once again became an issue, this time with our IT tech, Lee. Because of the usual computer problems every office has, I would often need Lee to debug or update or reconfigure or delete something.

Lee found me attractive. Now, in normal circumstances, I would find that flattering. But Lee lacked the normal human instinct for tact and distance and common sense. He had no filters. Lee would take every occasion he could to explain graphically what we could do together. He would tell me I needed to have one more fling before marriage. He was unrelenting and thickheaded and obnoxious.

On a base, where circumstances dictate that you can't get away, there wasn't much I could do. I needed my computer to work, and Lee was the only show in town. I couldn't get away from the guy and had to try to tolerate his steady stream of incredible comments.

I told him in very clear terms that his behavior was unacceptable, but it seemed to have no effect on him.

Shortly after a heated exchange with him, while we were walking toward my quarters one night, he apologized, and I thought I had made at least a small impression on him and would take a small victory of any kind just to get him to stop.

When we arrived at my quarters, he asked to use the bathroom, which I obliged. But after, he kept thinking of excuses to hang out, and I had to literally tell him to leave, emphatically and quickly. He never got the big picture.

Sometimes the most truly earth-shattering events can begin so mundanely. My diary entry for April 8, 2009, was simple: "I found out a ship in the Gulf of Aden, Somali waters, got pirated and a US crew that took the ship back over has one pirate in custody. Go Americans!"

Four days later, Easter Sunday, I was on my way to Mombasa, Kenya, part of a select NCIS team chosen to investigate what happened on that "ship in the Gulf of Aden"—an incident that grew quickly to attract immediate world attention and four years later became a popular movie starring Tom Hanks, *Captain Phillips*.

Of course at the time, such enormous implications were beyond me. All I knew was that my reputation from my work in Djibouti had established me as someone who should be there. And that was fine with me.

The *Maersk Alabama*, with a crew of twenty, had been headed to Mombasa on April 8, loaded with seventeen thousand metric tons of cargo, when four young pirates boarded it.

The *Maersk* crew, which had received antipirate training, quickly shut down control systems, but not before the pirates captured Captain Richard Philips and several other crew members.

As the *Maersk* drifted aimless, the pirates and the remaining crew played a cat-and-mouse game to regain control of the steering, which led to one of the pirates being captured by the crew, then escaping after an exchange for Captain Phillips went awry. The tense and uncertain machinations between the crew and the pirates led to a five-day hostage situation in which the pirates demanded a $2 million ransom and ended only after Navy SEAL snipers rescued Captain Philips from the enclosed lifeboat where he had been held and killed three of the pirates. The daring operation and dramatic rescue involved several US Navy ships and took the approval of President George W. Bush to carry out.

Chaotic, fast-moving, and confusing, the incident had worldwide implications, with some questioning the United States' use of force outside its borders. It needed investigating, and it needed clarity quickly. The NCIS, and my team, was called in quickly.

We joined forces with the FBI in Mombasa to begin the first stages of the investigation, which required, among other necessities, questioning crew members and the surviving pirate. It was heady stuff, I have to say.

The NCIS team arrived at the dock where the *Maersk* was tied up by eight in the morning after the snipers' shots put an end to the incident. But we couldn't start until the FBI arrived, which took another five hours. I couldn't help but be unimpressed by what seemed to be the sheer arrogance of a few of the FBI guys, but I guess that is to be expected.

Dockside, there was a media circus by the time we arrived, and I remember thinking I hoped my parents wouldn't see me on television and start to worry. I was just there to do my job.

Somewhere I have a copy of a news service photo of us leaving the *Maersk*, smiling, identified in the caption only as "investigators." As I look back at things now, at how everything turned out, that day could have been the absolute highlight of my NCIS career.

A baboon eating cereal in Djibouti, Djibouti, on February 18, 2009.

Just landed in Mombasa, Kenya, on April 11, 2009.

In Mombasa City, Kenya, on April 13, 2009.

USS Boxer *coming into port in Mombasa, Kenya, on April 20, 2009.*

Cheetah Refuge in Djibouti, Djibouti, on May 22, 2009.

CITATION TO ACCOMPANY THE AWARD OF

JOINT CIVILIAN SERVICE ACHIEVEMENT MEDAL

TO

ROBYN S. C. COLEMAN

Special Agent Robyn S.C. Coleman, Naval Criminal Investigative Service, distinguished herself by exceptionally meritorious achievement in the Joint Force Protection Activity, Combined Joint Task Force - Horn of Africa, from February 2009 through June 2009. During this period, Special Agent Coleman performed her demanding duties in an exemplary and highly professional manner. She was instrumental in the overall safety and mission success of Combined Joint Task Force - Horn of Africa. She helped develop a source network which resulted in increased productivity in Djibouti. She developed close relationships with the Djiboutian law enforcement and military officials ensuring continued security for Combined Joint Task Force - Horn of Africa and Camp Lemonier personnel. These solid relationships have allowed her colleagues to provide positive intelligence information on atmospherics in Djibouti. She also provided outstanding support to Combined Joint Task Force - Horn of Africa when forward deployed to Mombasa, Kenya, in support of an interagency effort to a high visibility national mission. She conducted a voluminous summation of interviews, preserved the crime scene and collected high-value evidence. Special Agent Coleman's steadfast devotion to duty, leadership, and professionalism significantly contributed to the success of Combined Joint Task Force - Horn of Africa and will have a positive and long-lasting impact on peace and stability in the region. Through her distinctive accomplishments, Special Agent Robyn S. C. Coleman reflected credit upon herself, the Naval Criminal Investigative Service and the Department of Defense.

FOR THE SECRETARY OF DEFENSE
JOHN E. SARCONE
CAPTAIN, U. S. NAVY
CHIEF OF STAFF, COMBINED JOINT TASK FORCE-HORN OF AFRICA

Citation accompanying "The Joint Service Achievement Medal" from Captain Sarcone.

This is to certify that

The Joint Civilian Service Achievement Award

has been awarded to

ROBYN S. C. COLEMAN

GIVEN UNDER MY HAND THIS   SIXTH   DAY OF   JUNE   , 20 09

COMBINED JOINT TASK FORCE – HORN OF AFRICA
COMMAND

J. F. SARCONE
CAPTAIN, U.S. NAVY

The "Joint Civilian Service Achievement Award" certificate from June 6, 2009.

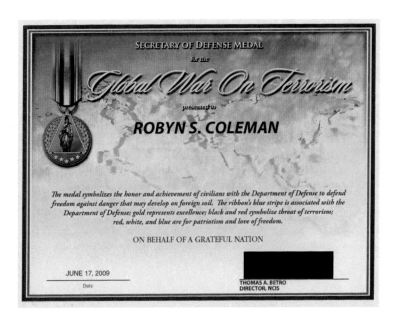

Secretary of Defense – "Global War on Terrorism" certificate from June 17, 2009.

Six

CAMP LEATHERNECK

My next tour presented me with challenges on several fronts, both personal and professional. It offered, if that was the proper word, neither the exotic charm of Djibouti nor the relative safety of Al Asad. That's because my next assignment was far more brutal and dangerous than anything I saw in Iraq. While Al Asad was in a combat zone, and caution and protection were watchwords for everything we did there, caution and protection took on a new and more ominous meaning for me in my next assignment.

I was off to Afghanistan, the stark, mountainous, and in places strikingly beautiful country that pushed me to new limits of learning about myself and my ability to adapt. My four months there, beginning in late December 2009 and into one of the deadliest years in American involvement there, provided ample opportunities to see and do things I would have preferred not to have seen or have done.

The four months also presented yet another experiment that tested my patience for dealing with male colleagues and supervisors who asked me to do strenuous and at times dangerous missions while at the same time managing to treat me as if I were a weak link, like a younger sister they were forced to babysit. It's funny how it kept working out that way. My optimism that eventually my record of accomplishments would overcome these preconceived notions never flagged. But it was beginning to dim.

In high school and college, I had heard about the so-called glass ceiling—what sociologists had described as "the unseen, yet unbreachable barrier that keeps minorities and women from rising to the upper rungs of the corporate ladder, regardless of their qualifications or achievements." By the time I was full bore into my career at NCIS, I honestly thought the concept of the glass ceiling was outdated. I felt that neither the fact that I was a woman nor the fact that I was a woman of color had much to do with anything. Those days were long gone, I felt. And good riddance.

I had no problems being promoted, nor with receiving citations for good work. But was that just smooth sledding in the early days? Would I be able to rise into management? Maybe head a mission overseas? It was too early to tell when I headed off to Afghanistan.

Afghanistan is an enigma that no foreigners had ever solved or subdued. Alexander the Great had tried and been repelled. The British made an attempt during the Great Game era of the 1840s, but their stay ended in 1842 when some five thousand British troops and twelve thousand civilian camp followers were massacred in less than a week after they left Kabul in what was understood to be a truce. Only one man of that ill-fated group survived.

In the mid-twentieth century and beyond, Afghanistan would prove to be an interesting and vital piece of the puzzle as the Soviet Union, China, and the United States curried favor with Afghan leaders. The Americans built a road here, the Russians an airport there, and the Chinese were everything. The last king of Afghanistan, Mohammed Zahir Shar, played the three superpowers brilliantly, gaining much improvement to his impoverished country but giving little away.

Then of course came the Soviet invasion in the 1980s and the Soviets' total humiliation as years of conflict showed just how resilient and brutal various Afghan factions could be when foreigners arrived. Post-9/11, post–bin Laden, American and NATO forces were learning the same lessons.

When I began my tour there at the austere, almost primitive Camp Leatherneck, the Americans and their allies were having a very difficult go at it. At Camp Leatherneck, in the chaos of Helmand Province, I was about to learn the harsh reality of life, and death, in Afghanistan.

I had left Djibouti sadly but buoyed in a way I hadn't felt in a while.

My experience there both professionally and personally was rich and fulfilling. Working with the encouragement and backing of Al McCreary made the hectic schedule I kept at Camp Lemonnier palatable. I felt valuable and valued, like a necessary part of a team that worked well together. Supervisors need to be confident in their ability to supervise—to make the most of the people who work for them. If they have that confidence, they can delegate without insecurity and can praise without petty jealousy. Al was such a guy.

In addition to the freedom of working under Al McCreary, I also took great pleasure in being free to get into town and to immerse myself in East Africa, which was stimulating near electrifying, I'd have to say.

Of course, going out with the *Maersk Alabama* investigation under my belt was a positive rush, and I'd be lying if I said it was nothing. I was credited with being part of the *Maersk* team in internal NCIS memos and reports, but my name was never made public, nor was it in any media coverage. That was good enough for me. Even though we were instrumental in the investigation, the FBI got the lion's share of the publicity. As always.

I also left Djibouti learning an interesting thing about East Africa dating, a cultural phenomenon quite different from anything in the West, where kids begin dating in their early teens. My friend Charika announced before I left that she had just broken off her two-week engagement, and she was almost blasé about it. There, no one dates until they are engaged, or rather as I understood it, you have to be engaged to even begin dating. So essentially she had barely known the guy she was engaged to before they started dating. I couldn't help but think this cart-before-the-horse approach would have been interesting with Nate and me.

▲ ▲ ▲

A big crowd from the office had surprised me with a going-away dinner in town the night before I left. It was a grand and delicious meal—spicy Ethiopian delicacies served East African style, with everyone sitting around the table and simply digging in, laughing and joking the whole night. Charika and Eli and Big Jo were among the crowd bidding me fond farewell. I thoroughly enjoyed it.

Later, many of the crew came to the airport to see me off on what I remember as an exceptionally hot day—which in Djibouti means *hot*—the thermometer at the airport hit 136 degrees that day. It was a terrific way to end an uplifting tour.

I came home to the usual frenetic mix of relaxation and chaos—all quite wonderful. Stepping off the plane after the predictably long and boring transatlantic flight into a misty Florida rain was refreshing and magical after all those months of unrelenting African sun and heat. But as with after my return from Iraq and Al Asad, I wasted no time. And this time I had new obstacles to overcome, not the least of which was finalizing my wedding arrangements. I also faced bidding on a new overseas assignment, catching up on maintenance I had to defer on my house in San Diego that was now occupied with tenants, more training, and getting ready to go back out.

It was a cycle I was growing comfortable with. I enjoyed the challenges and the uniqueness of being overseas, and it took very little time for me to start thinking about going out again. The cycle included days of near exhaustion at first, as if the four-month supply of adrenaline I had been running on in Djibouti was depleted—there was nothing left in my tank. This initial exhaustion had nothing to do with time changes either. When you're overseas, there is very little time to find genuine rest. I realized that when I came home to the States for the second time.

In Iraq and in Djibouti, I thought I was getting enough sleep, that my daily workouts at the gym and my care about what I ate would pull me through. But I was essentially on call twenty-four hours a day in Djibouti, and I thought I could muscle my way through it. But when I got home and had a chance to catch my breath, I realized how bone tired I really was. Being back in the States for a while was more than therapeutic; it was an essential antidote for burnout.

I had left Djibouti a single woman. I went to Afghanistan a married one, fresh from an astonishing and beautiful Caribbean cruise wedding and honeymoon. Nate and I married September 5, 2009, on Royal Caribbean's *Liberty of the Seas*. Thanks to Nate's friendship with a key NCIS higher-up, we both secured assignments to Camp Leatherneck, where we would be special agents not only at the large Marine base but as some smaller outposts that dotted Helmand Province—Camp Dwyer, Forward Operating Base Fiddler's Green, Camp Geronimo, Patrol Base Jaker, Lashkar Gah. Nate and I would be working together and living together in what I could only politely call stressful conditions.

If a good, solid marriage needs to start off slowly under low heat that will allow the main ingredients to blend at a simmer, gradually mixing to produce a solid and tasteful meal, Nate and I began our marriage zapped in a microwave under maximum power. I would not recommend four months in a lethal combat zone under continuous pressure as a way to start a marriage. Our time together in Afghanistan was interesting. And not always in the best way.

It took some adjusting, believe me.

Nate and I once again found ourselves with a few days in Kuwait awaiting final arrangement to get into Afghanistan. There, I was struck again by the wide cultural differences between the United States and our Middle Eastern friends: the exotic smells in the bazaars, the different forms of dress, the veiled woman and the cacophony of a different language being shouted at shopkeepers, the wafting Arabic music, the call to prayer for devout Muslims. Strange but inviting.

There was nothing inviting, however, about Camp Leatherneck, in the arid and truly hostile Helmand Province in the truly hostile country of Afghanistan, where Nate and I would spend the next four months.

I had almost innumerable and stark reminders of how far I was from Cincinnati and San Diego trying to find some semblance of sleep in a tent in the windblown desert, with heat often above one hundred degrees. At Camp Leatherneck, prime real estate was an air-conditioned makeshift plywood "cabin" that afforded at least a temporary break from the heat and the dust and the wind. Inside those things, I went to sleep almost finding comfort in the bare two-by-fours used to reinforce the quarters. The generators that supplied power to the camp were unpredictable, and blackouts were not what I would call unusual.

The first thing that struck me, that clearly hit me as we were flying in, was the color brown. The brown in Afghanistan is overwhelming, far from the formidable and green Hindu Kush Mountains that have protected the country from invasion for centuries. Brown is the prevailing color of the arid Helmand; though the province does offer slices of green near its canals and vivid red when its poppy fields are ripe for harvest, most of it is universally, deadeningly brown. We would often see media coverage using euphemisms like "sunbaked" that made the area seem almost attractive, like Arizona, but it wasn't. It was, and is, dusty and parched and tense.

Camp Leatherneck taken on its own was spartan, almost primitive. But then add the fact that it is set in the middle of one of the most hostile places on earth to be an American, a Ferengi, and throw in the additional information that Helmand Province is perhaps the world's most productive opium-producing area, and you might start to form a picture. But mix in also young, combat-stressed troops and men and women living together, and you have a volatile place to be a criminal investigator (aka special agent). The match was never far from the gasoline, in a manner of speaking.

And to put the icing on the cake, Nate and I had arrived at the beginning of what would be the deadliest year for foreign troops in Afghanistan since the US invasion in 2001. Many of these deaths were from improvised explosive device (IED) attacks on convoys and patrols. These patrols left Leatherneck almost continuously while Nate and I were there. And we know about them because our supervisor had no problem sending us out on what I felt were routine investigations that did not justify our lives. In two instances, in an effort to clamp down on drug use and sales by Marines at the camp, he sent us out to interview what I saw as small fish. He spent almost the entire time we were there trying to catch an Afghan he suspected was a major supplier of hashish and opium. He had no evidence that this guy even existed, and the problem of drug use on bases was actually minimal. But he tried nonetheless, and we could have easily been killed in one of these forays.

▲ ▲ ▲

In 2009, there were 7,228 IED attacks in Afghanistan, a 120 percent increase over 2008. The next year, with Nate and I making our excursions out from Leatherneck, there were 14,661 IEDs. These are brutal, sudden, and devastating attacks that can leave soldiers with debilitating lifetime injuries if they don't kill. The psychological effect was palpable. Soldiers going out on patrol always had the lethal possibilities on their minds. And back on base, that creeping tension could lead to other problems—crimes I often had to deal with and, even more shocking, suicides. Leatherneck was a grim and soulless place at times.

I was not a big fan of those statistics. With 496 casualties, 2010 was by far the deadliest year for US troops fighting a war in Afghanistan, according to casualty reports issued by the Department of Defense and tracked in a comprehensive database of war casualties maintained by CNSNews.com.

There were 303 US casualties in the Afghanistan war in 2009, making 2009 the second deadliest year of the war.

Almost seventeen times as many US troops were killed in the Afghanistan war in 2010 as were killed in 2002, the first full calendar year of the war. In 2010, US military personnel in Afghanistan were killed at a rate of about one every eighteen hours.

Marines had fought and died in Helmand for years by the time Nate and I arrived. It was and still is by far the deadliest province for the US-led coalition. There were also stories and evidence while we were there of heavy brutal combat. We'd watch the patrol leave regularly. And there were constant firefights, sometimes several a day, that we'd hear about. In fact, the Marines we'd talk to had a name for it: "Hell Man."

Our investigations were typical of any small, condensed area where stress was the order of the day: sexual assaults—not surprising given the mix of men and woman and the Afghan culture—and, for me incredibly devastating, many death investigations, a few from foul play, but many suicides.

There is nothing quite so unsettling, so deeply affecting and chilling, as seeing a dead body. In my work in Afghanistan, this discordant, truly shattering experience happened all too often. And the people whose deaths I investigated did not go quietly. The chaos that was Afghanistan in 2010 was so upsetting and so violent and so lethal it created a side business of its own. NCIS was charged with investigating sudden deaths. And I'm not talking about the all-too-many combat deaths outside, I'm referring instead to accidents and possible murders and, unfortunately all too often, suicides. I saw the bodies of too many young men who could no longer abide the stress and killing and pain and instead ended their own lives.

In training, we used mannequins to discuss physiology, and we used various scenarios and videos and gruesome photographs to understand what havoc is caused by a violent death and what it looks like. Those were our tools, our keys to understanding and completing a thorough investigation. We learned what a point-blank shot to the face would look like, what damage a strangulation might cause or a fatal knife wound.

But nothing in the classroom or a forensic science textbook can prepare you for the real thing. It promoted in me at least a mixture of nausea, fear, shock, and an almost out-of-body determination to be professional, to not let it show. But no matter how many of these investigations we went out on, I was never prepared, nor was anyone else on my teams. These were shattering experiences.

After one investigation of a young Marine who had shot himself in the head, under Cause of Death, I wanted to write "Loss of Hope" for that beautiful, faceless young man.

My own hope now is that I'd never get to the point where I'd view such horror as routine.

I did take comfort and solace in my faith, in my nightly scripture reading, which, as I look back now, covered many pages of my diaries of that time. I took comfort that these poor, tortured young men died for a reason and that no matter how violent their end or what pain they must have suffered to reach the point of killing themselves, they were at peace now. That is what got me through these things.

▲ ▲ ▲

In a country where women are kept under cover in purdah and away from the masses, Afghanistan presented some interesting challenges. At Leatherneck, as I mentioned, there was a mix of Marines, both men and women, and Afghan troops, many of whom were not used to such open and free relationships. This led to a number of assault cases, something I would learn all too personally in a later tour to that country.

Before I left for Leatherneck, while I was back in the States, I met a guy who had lived in Kabul in the early 1970s as a teenager. He gave me a quick glimpse into what Afghanistan had been like then for women and how Afghan men viewed them.

And he offered a bit of what I could expect from a culture that in many ways had not changed in hundreds of years.

He had attended the American school in Kabul in the early 1970s while his father was assigned to the embassy there. The American school played in a basketball league with other teams from Kabul including Kabul University, which catered to the children of the Afghan elite. Americans being Americans, when the high school team would play, they'd bring their cheerleaders, dressed as American cheerleaders would in short pleated black-and-gold skirts. And they would cheer the typical American cheers in gyms that would normally seat fifty people. Any game the American school played would have crowds over sometimes two hundred men, crammed in and gaping. It was like the equivalent of a live sex show.

Forty years later, the same attitude of Afghan men toward women still prevailed. They simply did not know how to act around women. And our investigations proved that. But I would also have to note that American men didn't know how to be around women either. And my own experience proved that.

That same guy told me another story about Afghan justice, which holds very dearly the concept of an eye for an eye. It said a lot to me about the local culture and about the Afghans we sometimes had to deal with. Or what we could expect if we were ever captured.

In 1971, an American nurse assigned to the embassy was murdered by her Afghan cook, strangled and presumably raped. The cook was arrested, tried, and convicted in two days and sentenced to be executed. This old hand's father represented the Americans at the execution as a witness. The cook had been hanged, he said. But rather than being dropped from a large height as is normally the case in such things, he was simply placed on a chair with a rope knotted around his neck and looped over a ceiling rafter. Then the chair was slowly moved away, leaving the man to die a painful and protracted death. Just as the nurse had. An eye for an eye. This was the culture I would be working in and the justice I could expect.

I didn't have to travel thousands of miles to the barren Helmand Province to learn that men might be threatened by confident women. I learned that in college in Cincinnati. The Afghans took it to a new level, though. In Afghanistan, they simply made them speak only when spoken to, never venture out in public without covering themselves head to toe, do every menial chore imaginable, produce children when necessary, and more than anything be deferential. I sometimes wonder if some of my male NCIS colleagues actually thought that was a good way to treat women as well.

When we were lucky (that is, when we didn't have to drive), we would often leave from Leatherneck in pursuit of investigations by quick helicopter flights that would zigzag over the arid patchwork of subsistence farms on our way to camps—outposts, they called them—that were even more spare than Leatherneck. We'd pass over the occasional dams and canals built in many instances by Americans or with American aid that had led one town in Helmand, Lashkar Gah, to be labeled "Little America" in the 1960s, so much did it model itself after SmallTown, USA.

Of course, that sentiment—or any sentiment that sounded nostalgic for America—had long since passed.

While I was there, I heard of a program that perhaps summed up the way I sometimes thought of our own mission there in 2010. That is, ill-planned and unlikely to work. Post-9/11, the United Nations, with the full backing of the United States and manned in many cases by Americans, had attempted to carry out a plan that would have local farmers stop cultivating the lucrative poppies that led to the lucrative opium market that produced a major amount of the world's heroin. Instead, the UN offered a chance to earn money by participating in Helmand public works projects like road and canal improvements. It was doomed, of course, from the beginning, for not only was the opium trade lucrative but many of these farmers were working for powerful local leaders. This was part of a traditional culture that an individual is first loyal to his family, which is extended then to his village, and then to his tribe. Then maybe to his country.

Certainly the Americans did not understand this concept, and it didn't figure into anything the military was doing as far as I could see.

What the military did that affected my life was to place young soldiers in harm's way with little chance to escape or relax or find some means to relive stress. And for the NCIS in Afghanistan in general, and for me specifically at Leatherneck and Camp Dwyer, Forward Operating Base Fiddler's Green, Camp Geronimo, Patrol Base Jaker, and Lashkar Gah, it meant crime.

But it meant in some odd way, despite the danger and the harsh conditions, another chance to prove myself. I worked on nine investigations independently and on many others with coworkers, including Nate.

Among them was an indecent assault involving a junior enlisted women and a man we could not, unfortunately, identify; an accidental death; several suicides; and a narcotics investigation involving multiple Marines.

In one accidental death I investigated, a Marine was using a chain hoist to lift one of the heavy tracked vehicles that were so prevalent in Helmand, so necessary to travel across the rugged terrain. He managed to lift the truck up and slide underneath just as the chain broke, dropping the truck and crushing him.

But these were in many ways routine cases, cases that really did not call for placing the investigators in harm's way, which in Afghanistan—in Helmand— meant being killed. Yet our supervisor there, whom I'll call Johnny, gave no thought to sending us off the camp to chase after what I felt were insignificant leads like the small fish in the narcotics investigation Johnny thought was so important. If Johnny could call attention to himself by bringing down a big drug bust, then all was well. If we happened to get blown to bits along the way, well, that was the price of war. And he pursued that quest with vigor almost the entire time Nate and I were there. He was obsessed with getting the small guy to get the big guy.

Johnny was this tour's challenge for me, what I would term was the headache of the whole operation. I guess you just can't escape these guys. Johnny was very controlling—a demanding micromanager who needed to take credit for everything that happened under his watch, even if he had nothing to do with it. At one point, I set up an entire outpost, under no small amount of duress, considering, first, that it was an outpost and thus not secure and, second, that it was a Helmand Province outpost, which of course made it even more insecure. Nonetheless, I procured all the furniture, set up the office, got the necessary computers and electronics, and arranged for the generator to power it all. It was an awesome and difficult assignment, and all modesty aside, I did an awesome job.

I heard nothing from Johnny, which was typical. He was the kind of guy who looked for things people did wrong so he could beat them over the head about it. In a way, hearing nothing from him was a sort of compliment. That meant, try as hard as he probably did, he couldn't find anything wrong with what you had done. He liked to make everyone who worked for him feel incompetent, to feel like a dumb kid. I have to admit that at times with me he succeeded. When you're under almost constant threat of death, that is no way to work.

I wondered how Johnny related to women on the outside. Did he expect his wife to take care of all the irritating domestic chores while he sat at home drinking beer and watching TV? Was he the type of guy who came home and expected the children to be clean and dinner to be on the table? I think he was. The question for me was how did these sorts of men rise to positions of responsibility? Later, I would be able to conduct some very personal research on that question at great cost to myself. The answer to that was they rose to positions of responsibility because they were promoted and lauded and patted on the back by guys above them who were exactly the same.

It's a man's world out there. But in Helmand I didn't realize it yet.

Shortly after we had settled in to Leatherneck, I got my first message that perhaps we were tempting fate to be there. The IED threats were almost continuous, and patrols leaving were on constant and nervous watch every time they ventured out. I kept wondering why we were dug in there and why Johnny wanted us to go out to several of the areas that were under attack. The day before, seven Marines had been severely injured, and we were all on edge.

Then it happened, an explosion so loud and with a force so great and immediate that we bolted from our tent in time to see a huge fireball just outside the camp. It was so close I was afraid for a moment that our tent would ignite.

Moments later, a British voice came over the loudspeaker systems announcing the blast had been a "controlled explosion."

There had been no warning. There was just an almost stupefying disbelief that they'd do something like that so close to the perimeter of the camp at a time like this.

"Sorry if there was some confusion," the voice added.

Another day, I was hit with another reality check. I had been in the middle of an interview for a sexual assault case when I heard a loud whooshing sound that prompted me to hit the deck immediately, instinctively. I felt we were about to be blown to bits by an incoming mortar attack. At that point, when I was still relatively new and fresh and sensitive, I guess, I felt as if I had never heard a more frightening sound.

It was an outgoing barrage, though. Nothing to worry about, someone told me. Sure, easy for them to say. I soon became so used to them that I barely heard them. And later I learned to distinguish incoming from outgoing, though that is not a skill I hope to use ever again.

And while Nate and I had our tensions, I absolutely cannot say enough about how superb it was to have him around in certain circumstances. Nate did make things much, much easier between males and females in our group. There were the usual amount of those tensions that arise everywhere and were not particularly unique to Leatherneck. What made them more pronounced, though, was Johnny, who seemed to have issues with every female. Nate was an absolute prince with the way he smoothed these tensions out for me and other females in the office when it came to Johnny.

There were some lighter moments, even in Helmand.

At one point, Nate and I went to do an investigation together on an entire unit of Marines at another base. When we arrived, our hosts wanted to put us in separate quarters, which is the typical way things are handled. But we insisted that we be put in the same quarters because the evidence we would be collecting would need to be in the possession of one of us at all times. And we told them we were married—something I'm sure they had heard before from amorous couples looking for a little time together.

When the time came for Nate and me to do our interviews and collect statements for the investigation, I would witness the statements with my hyphenated name. (Yes, I won the hyphenated name battle.) When the senior Marines helping us on the case reviewed the statements for later disciplinary actions, one noticed our signatures and said, "You are married! I thought you just meant married like you always work together like work husbands and wives."

We all laughed about that one.

And of course there were the UFO sightings. According to some of my colleagues there, a fair number of people at Leatherneck had reported seeing a series of "seven equally spaced lights" in the night sky over Leatherneck in March. I missed them, unfortunately, but it was a great topic of conversation later.

We needed diversion at Leatherneck in Helmand Province. It was at times the only way to make it through the long days and nights.

*Original NCIS office (left) and NCIS berthing tent (right) at Camp
Leatherneck, Afghanistan, on December 16 2009.*

Camp Leatherneck, Afghanistan sign.

Female latrine in the middle of an outpost base in Afghanistan on March 3, 2010.

A coworker and I pumping gas into an NCIS vehicle from a barrel and hand crank on March 29, 2010; unleaded gasoline was only available from barrels.

In traditional Afghanistan attire during a celebration at Al Asad on March 30, 2010.

"Naval Criminal Investigative Service Expeditionary Medal" for Afghanistan deployment from December 10, 2009 to April 4, 2010.

Seven

AND SO IT BEGINS

Heading back to Camp Lemonnier in February 2011, I felt I had become resilient and somewhat bulletproof. By that time, I was heading into my fourth deployment and had developed a solid reputation as a good, energetic, imperturbable special agent. I had investigated sudden and unpleasant deaths, sexual assaults, stalkers, robberies, drug deals. I had served as a peacemaker when cultures clashed, when interpreters and agents failed to get on the same page. I never flinched or blinked or cringed when the bombs and insanity became too much, when living in a glorified packing crate in the middle of the desert was the best it would get. Some people did.

I had been promoted and lauded and been sent out again to face the craziness and uncertainty of overseas work. Not everyone was cut out for the high tensions and gritty stress of close-quarters living. I actually enjoyed it to a point because it was challenging. I was learning. After eight years in the trenches, I was still confident. I was a veteran. I had acquired enough knowledge over the years at NCIS to know this without a doubt: I would never be invited to join the boys' club.

I would always be an outsider in that respect. The thing is, I didn't think it really mattered. And to tell you the truth, I didn't really care. I didn't have any desire to join the club and get my Guy Badge or secret decoder ring or whatever those boys in the club got. I hadn't done it in high school, when those sorts of cliques and clubs made at least a small bit of immature adolescent sense. I certainly wasn't going to jump on that boat as an adult. Heading back to Djibouti, I didn't think it would make a difference in my job and my life.

So here is the funny part about all that. I was experienced and hardened and knowledgeable, and I thought of myself as sophisticated in the ways of the world. But in many ways, I didn't know anything. I was naive about how things worked and about how strong I was. But I would learn, and all it took was two wrongheaded men in the wrong jobs at the wrong time.

My life would never be the same after my second tour of Djibouti.

In 2011, Djibouti hadn't changed since I had left there a year and a half before. In fact, it was all wonderfully similar and familiar when I got off the plane and saw that Big Jo had taken the time and trouble to get through airport security and be inside to greet me when I got through customs. The fact that I had somehow managed to get a seat in first class from Paris might have had something to do with my good humor as well. I managed to have a very relaxing flight courtesy of some nice first-class wine. Even the requisite crying baby a few rows back didn't bother me.

A few days in Paris had been refreshing, and I took heart in the fact that this time around, the City of Light was friendly and familiar. I was becoming a seasoned traveler, and I was enjoying that fact immensely. I felt I was part of Paris, not an outsider looking in, and that is the essence of truly learning to travel.

But while Djibouti and the home crew hadn't changed, I had. I was once again a single woman—-my marriage to Nate had barely made it past the one-year mark. Too many stresses too quickly and an Afghan honeymoon of sorts was not in retrospect the best way to start a marriage. Throw two newlyweds into the daily Helmand grind and compress the getting-to-know-you phase of any new marriage into a few short months surrounded by destruction and fear and bombs, all while trying to stay alive—I don't recommend it.

But somehow, more than anything, the time bouncing around the hell that was Helmand Province in 2010 had somehow tempered my resolve. It made me more aware of my own capabilities and my talent for getting things done without a lot of fanfare. I just put my head down and took things one step at a time. It had not been easy setting up Camp Dwyer. It had not been easy dealing with my supervisor Johnny's insecure indifference—just waiting for me to make a mistake so he could point it out and then take credit for fixing things. And it hadn't been easy seeing death so close, having to digest an almost daily diet of killing and maiming and young lives lost so violently and for a purpose I had yet to determine.

And it certainly hadn't been easy dealing with Johnny's anal-retentive micromanaging. He needed people to order around, to send on empty and pointless missions, because it made him feel important and powerful. You could see that he got great pleasure in telling people what to do. There was nothing anyone who worked for him could do—and I mean both men and women—that he couldn't and wouldn't criticize. He relished criticism and lived for it. But while he dished out his nearly always meaningless advice to everyone, he took greater enjoyment from making the few women in his command do more pointless things and take more of his orders than the men who worked for him. Was it because he was afraid some of the men would call his bluff? Talk back? Tell him he didn't know what he was talking about? I think so.

But I also took some pride in my relatively calm manner in dealing with his constant criticism, not just of me—and not just of the women who worked for him—but of everyone. Mind you, he was not a prince to the women, but he was almost an equal opportunity offender. The way he worked, the way he managed everyone, did make me wonder if there was a special place in quasimilitary situations like the NCIS that allowed this sort of bad behavior to flourish. I thought about whether there was something about that type of situation that allowed men to promote other men into positions of responsibility that they had no right or qualifications to occupy.

I had begun realizing with my increasing experience that the wonderful working relationship I had with Al McCreary during my first tour in Djibouti, the mutual respect and genuine appreciation of each other's roles and duties, was the exception rather than the rule.

But dealing with Johnny in the tense situation of Helmand, I thought, was a victory of sorts for me. I identified Johnny's ego problems and insecurity early, I pushed it from my mind, and I did my job. I made it, though, and I was praised for my work there.

Once I realized that Johnny's management methods were really a form of self-preservation for him, I became quite nimble at anticipating what he would criticize, and then I headed it off. If I heard nothing from him, I knew I had done a good job. But that's a hell of a way to work.

I had arrived back in Djibouti energized and I guess wrapped up in an air of confidence because I had not only survived but had excelled working with—or maybe around—the Colonel in Iraq, Johnny in Afghanistan, and—even what to me at that point seemed so far and distant—Daniel at the post office. I felt I could handle whatever hurdles management threw in my path. I knew I could do my job, had been promoted for doing my job well, and had developed a certain resilience for dealing with male supervisors who seemed to have never learned about equality of the sexes and the perils of gender discrimination.

I was not and am not a militant feminist by any stretch. I simply wanted to be judged on my performance, not how I looked and not how some men seemed to think women should act—quiet and respectful and subservient. Being brash and confident and assertive was considered a great set of qualifications for men, just not for women. I had never complained and had simply warriored on through some at times stunningly adolescent behavior from my managers. I could deal with it, I thought.

Was there something—a psychological oversight, perhaps—that had put so many men in positions of leadership when their overall maturity in dealing with women had never gone beyond the seventh grade? Some managers—not all—were like perpetual fourteen-year-old boys, unable to recognize that women had long ago stepped into roles of responsibility and competency.

I have come to believe that this mentality can thrive in the military and in organizations like NCIS, where ranks and protocol are so clearly delineated. Is there anything comparable in private industry? Where you are, by custom if not rigid rule, supposed to address your superiors as sir, to salute when you pass? In fact, where other than the military are certain individuals commonly recognized as "superiors"? Does not that imply in a way that, say, a twenty-five-year combat veteran sergeant is then inferior to a newly graduated ROTC second lieutenant?

I think the whole system can give people in positions of power an unusual sense of their own importance. In private life and industry, you wouldn't see a junior staff member strolling down an office hallway and snapping to attention to greet a passing CEO. Mailroom workers at Big Corporation ABC are not required to salute middle managers as they pass through. But they would have to if they were in the military. I think sometimes the ranks and the ribbons of the military and the quasi-military provide insecure leaders with the faux confidence and bravado to order people around whom they would never, in a civilian lifetime, be able to. In the wrong hands, a rank is carte blanche to bully, not lead.

Over the course of my years at NCIS, I was reminded on an almost daily basis of the Peter principle, a management theory that states that anything that works will be used in progressively more challenging applications until it fails. In hierarchical organizations, members are promoted to their highest level of competence, and then further promotion raises them to a level of incompetence, where they spend the rest of their careers.

Were my managers living proof of this theory?

A competent, even outstanding, NCIS investigator, for example, might be promoted to management, where he will reach his level of incompetence through no fault of his own. A really bright and enthusiastic NCIS investigator who becomes an incompetent manager could be set up to fail because firing government employees is so difficult.

The Peter principle also asserts that once they reach this managerial level of incompetence, they realize they are in over their heads and begin exercising what business analysts call self-protection—making sure that no one around them is perceived as being more efficient or, God forbid, better at the job they now hold.

When it was first proposed in the late 1960s, the Peter principle was offered as a somewhat wry and humorous look at how companies and bureaucracies can fail. NCIS is part of the government's civil service; it has ranks and levels you either rise through or stay in. It is very common for your colleagues to know your level, and just as in the military, rank trumps everything, even basic courtesy: He's a GS-14 and you're a GS-12. Too bad. Take your lumps. And add to the situation the outside pressures of Iraq and Afghanistan, and you have a recipe for some serious conflict if the players let it happen—or make it happen.

Applied to my own professional life in Iraq, and Afghanistan and Djibouti the second time around, I found nothing humorous about the Peter principle at all.

I'll admit that this might sound overly dramatic and might even sound a bit petulant, as in sour grapes that I didn't get my way. But that's not the case. It's just an honest assessment of things: power corrupts, and absolute power corrupts absolutely. Take the civil service and a little mix of the military, add the Peter principle, and you've got some problems.

I knew I did after my first conversation with my new manager in Djibouti, Jael Hintes, and then shortly after that with a second conversation with his cohort and colleague, Darius Bender. Bender and Hintes complemented each other in their indifference and insensitivity and total lack of understanding of basic human interaction—and for me, that did not bode well.

I knew I was going to be in for a ride unlike any other assignment I had. These guys were true pieces of work, macho ex-military men forged in the good old boys' network, then polished and refined in their self-absorption as they worked their ways up the NCIS ladder.

When Big Jo met me at the airport in Djibouti, I noticed Jael Hintes in the background in the middle of a flurry of activity. He hadn't come to meet me but was there on other business. He didn't come over to say hello at that point, and we weren't able to officially introduce ourselves or even talk. Now, normally it was considered customary courtesy for the ranking agent to greet every new-comer at the airport and welcome him or her aboard. That's what occurred on every one of my other overseas deployments. At the time, I thought he might have been busy and wrote it off. I certainly did not think him rude. Our first introduction, then, was silent and distant. As things progressed, that was the best it ever got. It was all downhill after that, and it didn't take long to get there.

My diary entry for February 9, 2011, my first full day back in Djibouti, notes: "I went to talk to Jael about some administrative stuff. We then had a falling out...Lord help me."

And that was just my first day of work back in Djibouti.

Hintes was the supervisory special agent in charge of NCIS operations in Djibouti. In the bureaucratic hierarchy, his number two was Darius Bender, the resident agent in charge. They worked together in offices that abutted each other in the small building that housed operations. It was in many ways a redundant arrangement, with in effect two supervisors. But that is the way the government can work at times, and for me, it meant twice the aggravation.

Hintes, short, bald, and bespectacled, was not a guy who spent a lot of time in the gym or doing anything that might in any way provide him with even a bit of fitness, and he sported an ample stomach as proof. The short, dark-haired Bender was a sort of Joe Pesci look-alike. To me, they seemed like two little terriers. They worked as a team in many ways, and not necessarily to good effect.

In any office, communication is key. In a textbook situation, managers know what they want, they inform the people in the office what is to be done, and they let those people—presumably people chosen for specific skills and initiatives and knowledge—do their jobs. Here is the goal. Accomplish it. Not so complicated in the right situation, correct?

Hintes and Bender were incapable of communicating even the most basic message. It was almost as if they conspired to deliberately live in a fog of confusion and short-circuited messages. I came to believe that if Hintes was about to be hit by a Greyhound bus as the two crossed a road, Bender would fail to tell him to jump aside.

And in their small, enclosed boys' club, no girls were allowed. If problems arose from mixed messages, in their view, it was because girls don't understand.

From my very first conversation with him, I knew that Hintes was not a listener, or rather I saw that he was the type of listener who heard only what he wanted to hear. I could almost literally watch what I was saying to him go in one ear and out the other. My relationship with Hintes deteriorated so quickly that at first I turned to Bender to be able to get my assignments done. I thought that if I reported to Bender what I had been doing for the record, Hintes—who worked five feet away from him—would have a record of my progress on various assignments.

But I realized, also quite quickly, that, too, was a bad idea because Bender would not relay information to Hintes. And Bender would often confuse information and mix up various things I would relay to him, so my efforts were in vain. Even though their offices were next door to each other's, they rarely talked clearly to each other—if at all. They were like two brick walls, mute and unmoving.

Shortly after I arrived, and after yet another argument with Hintes over procedure while Bender was present (both advised me to do something that was unprofessional at best and possibly unethical), I decided to communicate with each by email only. And in that small office, and in the confines of a small outpost in a small base in Africa, that system worked best because I had a paper trail of all the various mixed messages I had been getting from both.

And of course the fact that Bender had called me a bitch made the decision to start emailing all that much easier. Being called that made me feel like a child, demeaned. But that epithet was just the start of a steady and almost uninterrupted stream of harassment from both men. Once I had asserted my own competence and my unwillingness to acquiesce to their various and ever-changing suggestions, I had drawn the line.

I felt there was a creeping racial issue as well, because the only two agents in Djibouti at the time who were subjected to the often childish reprisals of Hintes and Bender—like making us repeatedly revise reports—were me and Kira, another woman of color.

Kira went through the same harassment, but over the first few weeks of it, I was much more vocal in my responses than she was. Kira was a new agent and was thus afraid of making too much noise and being tagged as a troublemaker. As a seasoned agent, I didn't care about that and felt Hintes and Bender should be held accountable for their actions. I truly believe that if I had been a supervisor, I would have been fired or reprimanded severely if I had done the same things those two did. It seemed managers could screw up time after time and still stay managers—or even be promoted: the Peter principle at work. It was not the same for agents.

So Kira essentially endured the same treatment and was actually called a bitch twice. I understood where she was coming from.

As a result of this harassment and the stress it produced, Kira's hair actually began to fall out, and in a relatively short time, she had a growing bald spot on the back of her head from the stress. But she never complained to anyone but me. We kept each other going every day, leaned on each other for support while this was going on.

The environment quickly deteriorated and became what I can only describe as hostile. It was like the proverbial Chinese water torture, one drip at a time until the simple task of turning in a simple report became so stressful that I started losing sleep, I started having stomach problems, and I started being overcome by a sense of anxiety that I had never in my life felt before.

As things got worse, both men did everything they could to make them even more so. I tried to avoid showing any signs that this boorish and bullying behavior was affecting me, but I couldn't. And like with a shark that smells blood in the water, if I showed a resistance or a weakness, they pounced on it.

At times when other agents had nothing to do, I would get an additional assignment, even though I might have three cases. When I handed in a report at the end of the day, I'd be given another one to do and be told to have it done by morning.

Other agents noticed, but few did anything to protest. I took no umbrage at that, because in an office like that no one wants to draw attention to himself. Why get the same treatment I was getting? A contentious office like that becomes a game of self-preservation in many ways—every worker for himself.

One sympathetic male colleague arranged with me to give Hintes identical reports covering a theft we had investigated on base. I mean identical, right down to the commas.

Hintes reviewed mine and demanded further information and corrections and said he needed the report back within two hours. He said nothing to my male colleague and accepted his report—if he read it at all.

From all appearances, Hintes and Bender enjoyed the game of bullying. After all, that was their job—telling people under them what to do and when to do it. But in my instance, for whatever reason, they enjoyed creating tension and then expanding it, twisting in the screw one more turn.

Toward the end, the stress got to me as well. They relished, absolutely enjoyed with great visible glee, creating additional reports and deadlines that left no time for me to seek some sort of solace from the two things I used to relieve stress: working out like a maniac at the base gym and going to church. No other agent had the reports and deadlines, and the constant screaming for corrections, that I did.

NCIS, as does any large organization, has avenues for employees who are upset or stressed or unhappy. My problem was that I was in Djibouti and counselors were in the States. I did try as often as I could to visit with the chaplain and talk to him since I couldn't seem to get in to see the NCIS counselor. The chaplain actually recommended I read Psalms and try to do things I like to do, like the gym and church.

I told the chaplain that I had been trying to do things like working out but that Hintes and Bender had told me they each thought I was going to the gym during work hours. That was how far it had deteriorated. They watched me every second of the day.

I still have notes I scribbled on a program from a rare church service I had been permitted to attend by Hintes and Bender. The notes show my state of mind and give a bit of a window into my struggle as I tried to take the high road with those two men, tried not to take their small-mindedness personally:

"Grudges hold people rather than people hold grudges."

"Forgiveness is a choice."

"An unforgiving spirit is like a prison."

"When you fail to forgive, you transfer that unforgiving baggage to someone or something else."

How did all this start? This petty recrimination that grew so large and so consuming that it took up every waking moment of my day and most of my fitful sleeps? How did it start so quickly? I had barely unpacked when the fight began. And it was a fight that I had no ammunition or preparation for.

The incident that started the entire struggle and the ensuing tensions was an alleged rape my second day back at Lemonnier involving two American soldiers on the base, a man and a woman.

The victim had initially been reluctant to press charges, but because she had confided in an officer in her unit, he in turn had notified NCIS. But there had been a delay. I had worked multiple sexual assault cases in the past and knew exactly the steps and protocol to complete an investigation. Hintes, however, immediately told me precisely how he wanted the case handled in a way that I felt was condescending and disrespectful to me professionally—and I told him so. I explained my skills and background in the hope that he would understand that while I was young in age, I was a senior agent and should be treated accordingly.

And so it began. Rather than apologizing for overstepping his authority, he took offense.

Then Bender stepped in with his own advice on handling the case, which led to not one but two of my supervisors providing me conflicting guidance on the same investigation. The two also began giving me what I knew was actually illegal advice and bad direction on the various steps I needed to follow in the investigation. One example of this was telling me to conduct interviews for screening possible suspects and witnesses by using a picture of the victim.

Just days before, a lawsuit had been filed against the Navy regarding the violation of victims' rights in sexual assault cases. I explained this to Bender and told him that conducting screening interviews is one thing, but utilizing her picture seemed immoral and was violating the victim's privacy.

Bender nonetheless demanded I obtain a picture of the victim and use it while conducting screening interviews. And in doing so, he once again made me feel as if my voice did not matter because I was a young female agent—like I was too young to know what's right when in fact I was trying to save them some embarrassment. This put me in a compromising situation.

So I went over his head and sought the advice of NCIS headquarters and was told I was correct in not using the victim's photograph—that doing so would violate her right to privacy. When I told Bender of that ruling, he immediately changed his tune and insinuated that he had known all along using the picture was a bad idea. It was as if he had some sort of self-protective amnesia.

This is what I was dealing with from him and Hintes on a daily basis. It was insane.

In another example of this sort of mismanagement, Bender told me to attempt to get internet records of the victim's activities from her personal computer. Not only would this be yet another violation of her rights, but legally we would need to obtain a subpoena to do so, I explained. Once again, he insisted, and once again, I went over his head to get a ruling. Once again, my instincts were upheld by headquarters, and once again, Bender pretended he had never made the suggestions in the first place.

By that time, I had firmly established myself in Bender's and Hintes's minds as a troublemaker. The war was on. And so began their constant monitoring of my every hour and my every action—always with the mind to find fault with anything and everything I did.

As the daily harassment continued, I went through accepted NCIS procedures standards and filed an EEO complaint with the next level, my overall supervisor back in the United States, who was at the time in Afghanistan. But that went nowhere and in fact backfired when he blamed me for being too pushy and assertive—good characteristics in a male investigator but apparently not in a woman. In the end, the in-house (informal) investigation into the various conflicts ended with an "inconclusive" finding...go figure!

It was not, however, inconclusive to me.

That's when I hired an attorney and filed a formal complaint with the Equal Employment Opportunity Commission. It was something I had never done before or even considered, but I felt my back was against the wall. It was a drastic step, and it was not what one would consider a prudent measure to ensure my continued promotions and a long career with NCIS. But I had reached the end of my rope.

I was infuriated by the informal investigation results and knew I had to take further steps to have my voice heard. It seemed I was all alone—but I felt I had the courage and whatever else it would take to stand up for myself and Kira. I really felt that NCIS should have had my back, and—naive or not—I was hurt that its informal investigation had in effect excused the behavior of Hintes and Bender.

Some of my fellow women coworkers urged me to file, and during the course of this discussion, I found a statement from a female agent, who had worked for Hintes previously, who had very similar issues with him, which made me feel I was doing the right thing. It made me feel these supervisors needed to be held accountable for their sexist ways.

By that time, I had worked six years as an NCIS agent and, including the post office, nine years for the federal government. Until that second Djibouti tour, I had never been treated as a second-class citizen and made to feel less of a person because I am a female. I felt that all NCIS agents were professionals who should be treated with dignity and respect. I had never been so often treated like a child unable to make her own decisions.

I had reached the critical, stress-filled point where I felt I could no longer breathe.

Camp Gilbert, Dire Dawa, Ethiopia.

A bathroom facility at a Djibouti Police Station I used on February 26, 2011.

Camels at work in Ethiopia on March 09, 2011.

Smiling camel in Ethiopia on March 10, 2011.

Eight

BREAKING THE CAMEL'S BACK

I t is ironic to me that the idiom "the straw that broke the camel's back" is Arabic in origin, because the whole tawdry, draining, debilitating situation originated in Djibouti, which has a heavy Arab influence. In the tale, a camel is gradually loaded down yet continues to function until the weight of a single straw brings him down. I'm not certain even now what the single straw was for me—which incident in a growing and continuous number of setbacks was the one that put me over the edge. Bender and Hintes had no shortage of ways to remind me they were in charge. If I didn't know that they rarely communicated anything between them, I'd almost think they had planned a tag-team assault on me. "I'll have Coleman redo her report for the fourth time, then you tell her to work overtime and stop going to the gym."

Was it the continued harassment while I was still in Djibouti and back at home in the United States? Was it learning that Jael Hintes was promoted after I filed my complaint? Was it my assault later in Afghanistan? Was it the informal finding that my EEO charges were inconclusive? Was it the lengthy and tedious EEO process? I will tell you this: there were a lot of straws, and for quite a while, I just simply brushed them off and went on with my job. That's the insidious part of harassment like this. It's cumulative. I could shake off one thing—I could shake off dozens of things, actually. But eventually it wears you down; it erodes your strength and your resilience to the point where you become paralyzed—without depth or humor or any sort of vigor.

101

But I kept at it. I worked as I always had, not knowing that my psychic bank account was almost to the point where I was overdrawn.

And at one point shortly after I returned from Djibouti, I did so well on a temporary assignment in North Carolina that my supervisors asked me to extend. To me, that says two things: I was still capable of doing my job and doing it well, and I did not yet know how badly the stress from Hintes and Bender had eroded my reserves.

But eventually it got to me.

Depression—and the numbness and pain and total crushing lethargy that it brings—doesn't arrive with bells and whistles. It doesn't come on with sirens wailing and flashing red lights. It comes slowly, and with it, depression brings a listlessness and lack of affection for life that sinks bone deep and embeds itself in everything you try to do. No matter how hard you try to move, to become involved, you can't. Depression creeps. It seeps into your soul, all the better to firmly attach its tentacles in your psyche. When you finally realize something is awry, it is too late, sort of like turning around and being hit with a baseball bat in the back of your head.

Frankly, very few people understand what depression is. I certainly didn't. Before it laid me about as low as I could get, I probably would have been one of those people to say to a depressed friend, "Just think about happy things" or maybe "Why don't you just go outside and get some fresh air?"

By the time I realized I might be in trouble, it was too late. I didn't need friends to tell me to cheer up or stop feeling sorry for myself or count my blessings.

I actually had a friend tell me to stop being so selfish, that I was just having a bad day, and perhaps I might have brought on some of the things that were troubling me all by myself.

No, I was not being selfish. No, I was not having a bad day. I was having a bad life at that point. And no, I brought on nothing by myself.

Depression for me built slowly and subtly, just like the actions of Hintes and Bender. It wasn't as if someone flicked on a switch and I found myself suddenly looking for help. As I look back on it, there wasn't a single remark that prompted me to file my complaint. There wasn't one truly ugly thing they said or made me do. It was an accumulation of things that built up gradually until I couldn't take it anymore—until I knew I had to do something. As I said, I never filed a complaint against Johnny in Afghanistan, nor did I take any action against the Colonel in Iraq. I just let it slide.

▲ ▲ ▲

I just let it slide. It seems so simple, like letting things slide is the right thing to do. Letting things slide in my case was like avoiding an oncoming hurricane by closing a few windows.

Maybe letting those things slide left me more sensitive to Bender and Hintes. Maybe some of the necessary thick skin I need to be a successful woman in a man's world had worn a bit thin.

And I must make it very clear that I doubt any of the men in my group in Djibouti would have been able to handle the steady stream of insults and demeaning comments and petty retributions. But we will never really know about that because Bender and Hintes's particular bile was reserved for the women in the group, especially me and Kira—who also happened to be a woman of color.

After I filed the EEO complaint but before I left Djibouti, headquarters began what they termed an "informal" investigation into my charges. As a result, quite a few of my colleagues informed me that they had my back, that they, too, had heard racist and sexist comments from both Hintes and Bender. Don't worry, they said, we will talk to any investigator and verify what you said. But I soon learned that "informal" took on an entirely looser definition. Even after Bender admitted he had called me a bitch, after my sympathetic colleagues were all interviewed, investigators found that any evidence for my charges was "inconclusive." When I asked to review the investigator's report, including any notes from interviews, I was told they had been "lost." I was furious, of course.

Both Hintes and Bender did not know that other members of our group in Djibouti had spoken to investigators, and they continued to deny everything. The fact that the investigation report's notes were "lost" did nothing to encourage them to apologize, and they never did. They just carried on as usual. After I left Djibouti, I never heard from either man again.

That was a possible straw.

Once I left Djibouti, I had no further contact with either Bender or Hintes, which was fine with me. I did not know what their responses had been to my EEO complaint. Nor did I care. I was happy to be out of there and happy to be away from them.

A bright spot, which I always welcomed, came after I served a temporary duty assignment at Camp Lejeune, North Carolina. There, I did what I always had done, which is take the initiative to conduct my own investigations, write detailed reports and recommendations for each case I was involved in, and report to a command group that respected what I did. In fact, they respected it enough to give me a NCIS Operational Excellence Award in August 2011 for the months I was there. I found that quite interesting. A few short months after Hintes and Bender found me incompetent and difficult to work with, I got an award—for doing what I always did and what I had tried in vain to do in the madhouse that was the Djibouti office.

The Lejeune assignment provided another bit of, I guess, vindication. Because of what he termed my "stellar" performance there, the officer in charge requested that I extend for another month.

What is funny to me is that I did nothing different.

Before I left the States for what would turn out to be my last overseas assignment, I read an email announcing that Jael Hintes had been nominated for a promotion—of course while my complaint was far from being settled. Do all things in a bureaucracy operate in a vacuum? Did anyone on the promotion board know that Hintes was the subject of a complaint that would cast serious doubt on his managerial skills?

His promotion was another straw, I guess. I took that as a major slap in the face, though. We agents had a running joke that you had to really screw up to get promoted. Many a truth is told in jest, I guess. But there was another of a growing number of straws.

It was upsetting enough that I immediately wrote an email to my attorney, Tracy Gaines:

Good Morning Tracy,
It seems Jael Hintes had been nominated for promotion. This is upsetting to me because it seems NCIS doesn't take complaints of discrimination seriously. I don't know how to take this.
Regards,
Robyn Coleman

Trying to help ease my irritation a bit, Tracy responded with this:

Robyn,
I'm sorry to hear this. It could be, as you suspect, the agency doesn't take your complaint seriously. It could also be that the individual(s) responsible for nominating him don't know about your allegations.
Tracy

But life carried on, and I remained enthusiastic if a bit battered about my NCIS career. I still had faith that things would somehow work out in the end and I would somehow be vindicated.

In March 2012, I found myself back in Afghanistan, back, in fact, at Camp Dwyer, the very base where I had helped set up the NCIS office. Much of what I had acquired and organized and set up was still there, which I found reassuring. I had never been one to look for pats on the back or constant praise. That was in part brought on by knowing that I did well—as my Lejeune supervisors had indicated. Normally, I wouldn't have given a second thought to how my office setup at Dwyer was basically unchanged. But Bender and Hintes had so undermined my confidence that I took great pleasure that someone must have liked my work.

I was prepared for the rigors and spartan existence of Afghanistan, which made the five-month tour there easier to take. Not that it was easy, mind you. It was the same inhospitable Helmand Province landscape playing host to the same carnage. If you take young Americans and drop them into a hostile and totally unfamiliar environment in which people every day would like nothing better than to kill them, you will create an almost unbearable tension. Place these same young Americans on a small base, and you will get crime. That is why NCIS has such a strong presence in Afghanistan, and that is why I was there.

And as it was during my first Djibouti tour with Al McCreary, and my supervisors at Lejeune—actually, as it was for most of my assignments—I had wonderful, respectful, and encouraging supervisors. They were truly great to work with—accommodating and energizing, always looking for the best way to help me conduct an investigation. It was, as I had always thought it should be, the way to run an office. It made the abhorrent management efforts of Hintes and Bender all the more obvious to me. It really made them stand out.

I realize now that while I was in Afghanistan, back at Camp Dwyer, all the many things that had gone on under Hintes and Bender were slowly brewing into a psychic storm that would erupt only later. The straws were piling up.

The icing on the cake, perhaps the last straw, was that I was myself the subject of a sexual assault while I was over there. Ironic, I guess, that after all the many sexual assaults I had investigated, I'd have to call in a report about myself.

▲ ▲ ▲

One afternoon in July, shortly before I was to head back to the States, I was returning from a workout at the Camp Dwyer gym when I stopped by a nearby bazaar to see if I could buy some colorful Afghan scarves as gifts. A young Afghan named Bashear told me he had them for sale and asked me to step into the large former shipping box he was using as a stall. Bashear, I would guess, was about twenty years old, with dark black hair swept back in an Elvis pompadour. As we haggled over prices—an Afghan tradition—Bashear wrapped a scarf around my head and neck. When he reached to remove the scarf, he slowly and firmly squeezed my left breast. I immediately asked him what he was doing, and he said, "Just showing you a scarf."

As I turned to walk out, he grabbed my arm and tried to pull me closer to him, as if he wanted to kiss me.

"Come here, baby, come on," he said as I pushed him away, strongly and emphatically. I did what I had told others in my situation to do. I filed a report and I moved on, thinking that the unfortunate and repulsive incident would have no effect on me later. But I think now, as I write this, that it did have an effect on me. Bashear was disciplined, forced to move his goods from the bazaar, and cited in reports to other Americans as someone to be avoided. Case closed, I thought. But maybe this was another of the silent, lingering negatives in my life. They add up.

▲ ▲ ▲

During the five months I was back in Afghanistan, the EEO complaint continued to make its way slowly through the system. My attorney, Tracy Gaines, pretty much handled everything, kept me informed, and made things as simple for me as they could be considering I was on the other side of the globe.

Complications were inevitable, it seemed. Shortly after I arrived at Camp Dwyer, I received the first of what would be two affidavits from the Department of Defense investigator Cindy Mullen. Normally, the questions asked in this affidavit would have been asked during a face-to-face interview. Because I was not available, I instead had to respond in writing, which ultimately produced a sixty-six-page single-spaced typewritten response. And I was required to do this on my own time, off duty, and under a very strict deadline.

The instructions for me on filling out the affidavit were very clear, as were what I felt were the implications: "Be very specific and make sure you don't miss the deadlines."

You being the Complainant must have direct related information regarding the action(s) under review which will be helpful toward reaching a just and equitable resolution in this complaint. As such, you are requested to assist in this investigation by responding to the attached list of questions to the extent of your knowledge and ability and in as much detail as possible.

Please focus on known facts and circumstances, rather than speculation or opinion, and ensure that each response is clearly identified with the corresponding question should additional space be required. Please note that you should not limit your response to these questions only, you may provide additional information that you believe is pertinent to the matter at issue.

Since the complaint potentially could be elevated to higher appellate authorities outside the Agency, including the Federal court system, it is required that your response be submitted in the form of a sworn statement. **Therefore, after preparing your response (preferably type written) (1) note the number of pages in the lower left corner, (2) initial each page in the lower right corner, (3) sign the**

last page, and (4) convert the document to a .pdf or scan a copy and send via email to XXXXXXXXX.

Failure to provide information by the above suspense date will not stop the investigation, but may result in a report of investigation being issued based on the information that was available at the time. Your response will also be considered as your final statement in the IRD investigation unless changes are made prior to the suspense date.

Please be aware that at your option you have the right to consult a personal representative to help you prepare and present your response. However, before responding, please note that the information you provide is taken without pledge of confidentiality. The information will be released to persons within and outside the Agency (including Complainant) who have a need to know in order to resolve the complaint.

Additionally, the investigative file as a whole must be safeguarded in accordance with the Privacy Act of 1974 (Public Law 93-579). Thus any information contained therein (including the information you provide) should not be discussed or shared with persons not having an official need to know.

Please be aware that your response is appreciated and is critical to the proper disposition of this complaint.

Filing the complaint itself was stressful enough. The reprisals brought from Hintes and Bender cranked the stress level up a bit more. Answering those questions in Afghanistan under pressure brought out a lot of what I had been trying to keep at bay, trying to ignore. I cried in my room a lot.

Shortly after I finished the first affidavit, Cindy Mullen sent a second, this one requiring an additional forty pages of answers again under very strict deadline pressures. I filled it out but was highly upset. The obvious questions arose. Would the investigation of my charges be dropped because my answers were insufficient? Would it be dropped on a technicality, for example, because I missed a submission deadline?

I actually started thinking, Hey, give me a break. Why would you wait until I deploy to Afghanistan to send me not one but two affidavits to complete in a short period of time? I had to and very much wanted to continue my workload and not let my EEO affect my normal duties. As a result, I spent a lot of late nights in the camp coffee shop completing the affidavits in solitude.

I relayed my concerns to Tracy Gaines, and she made it very clear to Cindy Mullen that my situation in Afghanistan was highly unusual and that in effect I should not be penalized for doing my job overseas.

Ms. Mullen,

Attached please find Ms. Coleman's completed, primary affidavit. Ms. Coleman and I both worked as diligently as possible to provide it in accordance with the deadline you specified. I trust the few hours delay is not meaningful given that they occurred during nonworking hours. Please note that, while the affidavit is complete, Ms. Coleman has not yet signed it. We need your guidance regarding this matter. Logistical problems in Afghanistan prevent Ms. Coleman from printing it, initialing every page and then scanning or faxing the whole thing back to you. I believe, however, that she can print and sign the last page. If that is not sufficient I could also have her add a statement saying that she is unable to initial all pages by hand, but indicating that she has done so electronically and attests to the accuracy thereof.

We are now working on the supplemental affidavit/interrogatories you gave her and will provide them as soon as they are complete.

Tracy Gaines

I never told my supervisors in Afghanistan about the complaint because I wanted to be treated fairly. It's a shame that I had to be so cautious, that what I went through with Hintes and Bender was such an aberration of acceptable NCIS behavior, so outlandish, that I couldn't share it with others. But it wasn't that outlandish, I guess, and it wasn't so unusual. So I kept my mouth shut and my head down.

I felt if I told them there was a chance they could have treated me differently. All I wanted to do was to get through my four months at Dwyer in peace, do my job well, and go home.

I had learned by then that once you file an EEO, the worry and pressure that comes with it won't stop: What will happen next in the process? What sort of surprise is waiting for me at the next turn? I felt that as soon as I got through one thing related to the EEO, something else was waiting to haunt me. I prayed to God almost constantly to keep me sane. And grew to hate checking my email or answering my phone because I was afraid of what I would have to answer to next. I was always on edge and had many sleepless nights.

I coped by talking to my boyfriend Byron, who is now my husband. He was an integral part of getting me through the EEO process, and his support was key to getting me through everything. I complained and cried to him a lot. I also just prayed and kept the faith that God was not going to put me through anything I could not bear. I must admit there were very dark times.

I had a glimmer of hope and vindication. Tracy wrote:

…wanted to give you one of the highlights (or, more aptly, low lights) from the ROI. Obviously, Kira will be an excellent witness for you. But, the best witness will be Timothy Andrews, who revealed the following, which he says he never told you or Kira (probably to protect your feelings): (1) Shortly after you were assigned to the office, or he learned of your assignment, Hintes rhetorically asked Andrews, "How am I supposed to run an office with all black females." (2) Upon learning of the assignment of an African-American, female AFOSI Agent, he commented "That's another black female." (3) Hintes later stated he planned to call HQ or CRFO about so many black women being assigned to NCISRA Djibouti.

I got through the second affidavit and let Tracy Gaines handle things after that.

Shortly after I returned from Afghanistan and Camp Dwyer, we got what appeared at first blush to be a victory. But it was shallow. A judge in the case ruled in my favor in the complaint and offered me a default judgment, the first positive sign that my complaint was justified, that Hintes and Bender had engaged in a systematic pattern of abuse and harassment that was unjustified and harmful to me.

Tracy's note to me read in part:

This is very, very, very good news. Default judgments are truly rare. This means that, as a sanction for the Agency's failure to meet its deadlines, the Judge has found in your favor in your case and is only holding a hearing to establish the amount of damages to which you are entitled. This means that we won't spend the next 6 months to a year preparing for a hearing to prove that you were subjected to harassment and you won't be spending tens of thousands dollars to try to prove that at the hearing. Instead, we only have to prepare for and have a hearing on damages. And, the whole time we are preparing for that you can rest secure in the knowledge that every penny of your legal fees will be reimbursed. I can't emphasize enough what truly wonderful news this is. And, the timing! You needed some good news with everything that is going on right now! I'm so glad for you!! Now, we wait, to see what the Agency does. I suspect it will have some sort of response and/or request discovery on damages, but we'll have to see. Tracy

But the reprisals began again as well. My victory was short lived and hollow, and it would have repercussions far beyond my career at NCIS, or what was left of it.

▲ ▲ ▲

Shortly after learning of the default judgment, I began planning for my next assignment in Washington, DC, and I was looking forward to it. I had the movers at my house in Georgia, I had planned a nice vacation with Byron, and I had a wonderful family reunion with my parents. For the first time since I had filed the EEO complaint, I was actually looking forward to something and excited about it.

Then came the phone call from headquarters. With my parents in town on a visit and while I was still on vacation, management ordered me back into the office. I was put on limited duty and charged with being involved with something I had nothing to do with. In fact, my only mistake had been traveling with someone who had actually done something worthy of punishment, though I did not know about her mistakes at the time. But guilt by association was apparently good enough for management—and good enough to somehow deflect the default finding against them.

That was the final straw.

My brief respite was over. It was starting all over again, and this time they managed to humiliate me in front of Byron and my parents. I simply could not take it anymore. I went back into the office, cutting my vacation short and upsetting plans I had with Byron and my parents. That is what a dutiful employee does. I was put on what they call "limited duty," really handcuffed in what I was able to do.

But I had by then been painted with a broad brush, tainted. I was a troublemaker. I was a whistleblower. I was a terrible employee and not a team player.

After that, things began to change. Suddenly I would realize I had been sitting on the couch for hours doing nothing. Or I'd want to make a cup of coffee but couldn't summon the energy to walk to the kitchen. I'd wake up occasionally with my heart pounding so hard I thought it would burst from my chest. I found myself unable to do even the simplest things, like go to the mailbox. God forbid if I had to go outside in the sunlight and actually interact with people.

I actually thought very briefly of suicide. Perhaps even a more dramatic sign that I was close to losing hope was that I stopped going to church.

Once they put me on limited duty, I sought counseling and never went back. It seemed to me there was no reason to go back, nor did I want to. Once the harassment began again, I went to a therapist who said I was suffering from both depression and anxiety and told me I needed to stop work, to get away from the things that were causing the problems.

With that diagnosis, I could no longer carry firearms, nor was I permitted to carry out the investigations that had been my lifeblood for so long, and I was put on medical leave. And though I was away from the fray, sitting at home pondering my next move if not my entire future, I was still always on edge about what reprisal NCIS had in store for me next.

Under those circumstances, my abilities to perform my job as a special agent were questionable at best. I still wanted to try, though. While on medical leave, I requested reasonable accommodations from NCIS in an attempt to go back to work in some capacity, but I was denied and told they couldn't accommodate me.

Disability retirement was my only option. I resigned in December 2012 to seek disability retirement.

NCIS "Operational Excellence Award" from August 28, 2011.

DEPARTMENT OF THE NAVY
NAVAL CRIMINAL INVESTIGATIVE SERVICE
FIELD OFFICE CAROLINAS

IN REPLY REFER TO

12450
Ser CAFO/11U263J
17 Nov 11

From: Special Agent in Charge, Naval Criminal Investigative
        Service Field Office Carolinas, Camp Lejeune, NC
To: Special Agent in Charge ▮▮▮▮▮▮▮, Contingency Response
        Field Office, Glynco, GA

Subj: OPERATIONAL EXCELLENCE AWARD

1.   It is a pleasure to commend Special Agent Robin S. Coleman,
for her support to Naval Criminal Investigative Service Resident
Agency Camp Lejeune General Crimes Squad. Special Agent Coleman
performed her duties in the highest traditions of law
enforcement and her actions exemplify the spirit of cooperation.
She is a credit to the Naval Criminal Investigative Service and
I join my colleagues in expressing our gratitude for all she did
to help accomplish the mission.

CHARLES T. MAY, JR.

Copy to:
CorrFile

NCIS "Operational Excellence Award" letter from November 17, 2011.

F.O.B. Geronimo, Afghanistan, on March 19, 2012.

F.O.B. Marjeh, Afghanistan, on April 16, 2012.

Cockpit in unmanned helicopter, Camp Dwyer, Afghanistan, on April 29, 2012.

Camp Dwyer, Afghanistan, on May 6, 2012.

"Non-Article 5 NATO" award certificate "for service with NATO"
from the period of March 11, 2012 to July 10, 2012.

AFTERWORD

There is a great wave of warm, embracing comfort in knowing you have done the right thing despite the heavy consequences. I certainly paid the price for filing my complaint against Hintes and Bender. It took a toll on my health and my psyche, and I must still be vigilant about what I do and where my thoughts wander to prevent myself from returning to the darkness that seemed to enclose me when I was at my worst. But I am vigilant, and I don't go there, and today my life is full of so many promises.

I had to leave a job I loved—one that I excelled in. I went through two years of trauma and uncertainty and continuous tension all because I stood up for what was right. And after all that, there were no repercussions for Hintes and Bender. In fact, Hintes was promoted. After all that, there were no institutional changes to the way women are treated at NCIS. After all that, things went right back to normal in the good old boys' network.

I haven't forgotten, but I don't live in it. Along the way, I learned an important lesson: look back at the past, just don't stare.

If you don't look back, you will never be able to learn. But if you allow yourself to be trapped in the past, you will never move forward. I know that I did everything I could and left nothing unturned in my efforts to call attention not only to the abhorrent behavior of Hintes and Bender but to the institutional mind-set that allow women to be treated like people of lesser value and intelligence. I take great satisfaction in knowing I tried to prevent the type of behavior exhibited by those two men—and by the men who looked the other way while it was going on—from ever happening again to other women in other NCIS offices.

After I left NCIS, I made a conscious decision not to allow Bender and Hintes to occupy any of my thoughts, and they haven't until I sat down to write this book. I don't mind temporarily revisiting those horrible days because I still hope something good will come out of it. After I left NCIS, I also decided that I would not permit the institutional malfunction of the men's world of NCIS and other groups like that to affect me personally. I made a conscious decision to simply accept what happened, call attention to it, and move on. I hope by sharing my story that I wake someone up, that I help another woman in a similar situation.

I am not going to bury it and let the status quo continue, where women are still treated like office assistants and coffee-getters and junior members of the club who should speak only when spoken to. That is why I have written this book and why I hope it will open eyes to the fact that even in the supposedly progressive twenty-first century, these things still exist.

And if that can help one person, revisiting all these very painful moments is well worth it.

I took some small comfort in the announcement in May 2014 that Defense Secretary Chuck Hagel was ordering the Air Force, Marine Corps, and Navy to reinvestigate hundreds of sexual assault claims that had been found to be without merit. Hagel took these steps after an Army reinvestigation found substantial merit to charges against nearly six hundred soldiers.

In other words, many sexual assault charges had been routinely dropped, and until a clamor arose about the dramatic increase in these charges, no one was paying attention. It was, as it always had been, a man's world. While the charges Hagel had concerned himself with were primarily physical assault charges, it does not take a huge leap of faith to understand that the type of mental and psychic harassment Hintes and Bender put me through was not unusual.

Hagel and the Pentagon had been prodded by legislators on Capitol Hill as well as advocates for sexual assault victims to change the way it treats victims and prosecutes offenders. That's what it takes to make change—outside influence and public attention. And that is why I am speaking out.

In August 2012, after the strains of Djibouti met the stream of continued reprisals from headquarters and combined with the daily horror of another tour in Afghanistan, I was diagnosed with major depression, generalized anxiety disorder, and posttraumatic stress disorder. As bad as that sounds, I'm not certain even today if that was the low point.

I could not continue to work, that was certain. The medications prescribed for the slew of conditions I had acquired left me unable to drive, dizzy, and almost continuously fatigued. I could no longer work out or go to church or go dancing with my friends. I certainly could not perform the job that only eighteen months before I had excelled at. There was no way I could carry a firearm and clearly no way I would be able to face the often-gruesome crimes an investigator has to deal with. I was concerned, as were others, that I might be a danger to myself or to others when I was under the fog of the medication. But being on the medication helped me to cope and have a sense of normalcy. It controlled the ill thoughts creeping in my head and the daily nightmares I had, where I would thrash and kick in the middle of the night.

I had no choice but to resign and hope to qualify for some type of disability retirement. I had always been a planner. Even in college I had a career plan when most of my friends didn't know what they would do the next day, let alone the rest of their lives. I worked hard at my plans, and I grew with them. My career with NCIS followed a steady path up the career ladder. I got promotions and raises and better jobs and more responsibilities with each passing year.

Resigning because of a disability was not part of my plan.

Shortly before I resigned, my lawyer—from the Kalijarvi, Chuzi, Newman, and Fitch Law Firm—reached a settlement with NCIS regarding my EEO complaint. By mutual agreement, the details cannot be released. At first, I had been satisfied with it, taking it as a small but satisfying victory in a long and rancorous battle that had taken a heavy toll on me. Today, because my confidence and my love of life and my energy have returned, I look at it a bit differently. Today I regret jumping at the settlement so quickly because I realize it was the final effort of NCIS to simply sweep things under the table. As I think about it now, had I chosen to carry the issues to a hearing, what I went through would now be a matter of public record. Maybe that might have helped, because even now I still don't think NCIS really cares about my harassment, and I am sure the harassment continues between managers and subordinates.

After I resigned and decided to apply for a disability retirement, I moved to Florida and stayed with a close friend—to try to simply regroup and enjoy some semblance of a newfound freedom. That is really what I look at as the first page in what would become a new chapter in my life. And that life, I said to myself in Florida, would never include working for the federal government again. Ever.

In Florida, for the first time in close to two years, I felt almost elated at times to be able to do whatever I wanted and not cower in fear, worried about some sort of reprisal. It was liberating.

At the suggestion of my therapist, I rescued a dog to help with my continued battles with depression and anxiety. Charley is a miniature pinscher mix, and he continues to be a blessing—my little protector even today. If someone comes to the door, he'll let me know, and as dogs somehow intuitively know, he simply understands when I need comforting in an almost uncanny way. After NCIS, I had for months felt vulnerable and helpless, and I'd look up and there was Charley—jumping on my lap and licking my face or just doing silly things to make me laugh. Charley is truly a joy.

After my Florida interlude, I moved back home to Cincinnati and stayed with my parents—this time at the recommendation of my doctor, who felt that the familiar warmth that only my mom and dad and sister could provide would help me with the still nagging depression and anxiety that I just couldn't seem to shake.

While at my parents', I began to feel organized and directed enough to write to my Ohio congressman and two senators—and to Vice President Joe Biden—explaining my situation: the effect of the harassment, my medical conditions, my lack of a disability settlement, and what seemed to me the inordinate amount of time it was taking.

In my letter to Biden and others, in fact, I pointed out that despite the serious physical and mental effects that entire issues had brought me—and the abrupt end of my growing NCIS career—one letter I received regarding my situation stated: "We realize that your condition prevents you from some types of work, but it does not prevent you from doing other work that is simple and routine." Very sympathetic, I thought. Sure.

But something worked.

Two weeks after I wrote Biden, my congressman, Steve Chabot, wrote to tell me they would "look into it." It was approved in October 2013. I was now officially retired and able to pursue an idea I had often toyed with over the years: starting my own business. And with that in mind, I moved back to the Washington, DC, area with Byron and Charley.

My first real tax-paying job was working for McDonald's on Boymel Drive in Fairfield, Ohio, when I was fifteen years old. While it wasn't the most prestigious job, it was the best job I ever had, hands down—even to this day. And what made McDonald's so great was the team—I loved the crew I worked with. Because of this encounter with McDonald's, I want to recreate that awesome work experience. I want others to have that same enthusiasm and camaraderie I had at McDonald's—that is what I strive to accomplish in my own entrepreneurial endeavors with my employees.

Counter that with my NCIS experiences working for such poor managers, and my idea really took off. I want to employ between ten and fifteen people and to make their work experience inviting and challenging and exhilarating. I want them to *want* to come to work each day, to think, I can't *wait* to get to work each day. I want to treat people with respect and dignity, to allow employees to grow personally and professionally.

I am doing this with my loving parents with the financial goal of allowing them to retire. I'll manage the business for free with all equity from the business going to my parents. After all, I think success should not be measured by the money you make but those you inspire along the way; this is something I strive for every day in my actions and even with writing this book.

In 2014, this business aspiration became a reality with a restaurant franchise in the Washington, DC, area. I managed a staff of ten to fifteen employees, and the vision of the team experience came to fruition; it was great for a while. However, the financial constraints of operating a business forced me to close a year later. It was disappointing, but this has not stopped my entrepreneurial vision. God willing and if finances allow, another inspirational venture will come along.

▲ ▲ ▲

Byron and I married in the summer of 2014, and our first child together was born in October 2014; a second child followed in 2017. Throughout the struggles and the travels and the trauma, Byron has really been there for me and has truly been a blessing; there are still many days when he carries me to the light with his candor and humor. I love him dearly.

We plan to focus on our family as partners and strive to be the best we can be together. My recovery process is an ongoing battle. It took a while to figure out the right combination of medications to keep me on track, which needs tweaking occasionally, but the combination of medications coupled with therapy has really been positive. Therapy is a great outlet and in my opinion should be a part of everyone's self-care regardless of need. The tools learned in therapy have really helped me to realize I have worth and I am resilient. I wake up happy every day because I am truly blessed and thankful that I will *never* have to work for another insensitive, hurtful, product-of-the-bureaucracy supervisor again.

Made in the USA
Monee, IL
11 October 2024

e8b266d3-afca-492b-8502-445924ca6babR01